EVANGELICALS
IN
AMERICA

Other Books by the Author

EVANGELICALS IN AMERICA

WHO THEY ARE, WHAT THEY BELIEVE

RONALD H. NASH

Abingdon Press / Nashville

EVANGELICALS IN AMERICA

Library of Congress Cataloging-in-Publication Data

NASH, RONALD H.
Evangelicals in America.
Bibliography: p.
Includes index.
1. Evangelicalism—United States. I. Title.
BR1642.U5N37   1987   280'.4   86-22241
ISBN 0-687-12177-9

All scripture quotations are from The New International Version. Copyright © 1973 by The New York Bible Society International. Used by permission.

MANUFACTURED BY THE PARTHENON PRESS AT
NASHVILLE, TENNESSEE, UNITED STATES OF AMERICA

To my wife, Betty Jane,
for her love and
support

ACKNOWLEDGMENTS

Several individuals were kind enough to offer suggestions and corrections as this book neared completion. They include Carl F. H. Henry, Robert K. Johnston, and David Beck. I appreciate their help.

PREFACE

This book has been written for the express purpose of filling significant gaps in available discussions of the American religious movement known as *Evangelicalism*. This book is designed to be a short, non-technical introduction to Evangelicalism in America. As such, it differs from other studies in several ways. For one thing, it is addressed to people who may not be evangelicals and who want to know more about this rapidly growing segment of American Christendom. The book tries not to presuppose any advanced training in theology or biblical studies. It also attempts to avoid some of the more technical questions that can sometimes arise with subjects of this kind. Where such questions could not be avoided, the book tries to keep the discussion as simple and non-technical as the subject will allow.

In addition to its usefulness as a source of information for general readers, the book is suitable as a supplementary text for college and seminary courses that include a short unit on Evangelicalism. It may also be helpful to church study groups that are interested in knowing more about this increasingly important religious movement. Large numbers of laypeople want to keep informed about what is going on in the contemporary church. They may read about the evangelicals in magazines, such as *Time* and *Newsweek*, or they may see a prominent evangelical leader interviewed on ABC's "Nightline" or on the Phil Donahue Show. People may keep tuning in evangelical television shows, like "The 700 Club" or the more typical television services of Jerry Falwell or James Kennedy. Their children may have encountered representatives of such evangelical parachurch organizations as Campus Crusade or Inter-Varsity. They may be curious about how Billy Graham differs from Jerry Falwell. In short, informed people need answers to lots of questions that can be asked about Evangelicalism. One purpose of this book is to offer answers to many of those questions.

For those scholars who read this book, one reminder is necessary: I did not write this book specifically for them. It is intended to serve as an introduction to a very complex religious movement. Its primary audience, therefore, is the non-specialist who wants to know more about Evangelicalism in America.

CONTENTS

EVANGELICALS
IN
AMERICA

CHAPTER ONE

The Evangelical Resurgence

The meaning of the word *evangelical* has evolved over many centuries to the point at which it is, at least in the United States, the contemporary term used to refer to theologically conservative Protestants. Only recently has the word also come to be applied to a small but growing number of Roman Catholics. One can normally expect that anyone who claims to be an evangelical is a Christian believer whose theology is traditional or orthodox, who takes the Bible as his or her ultimate authority in matters of faith and practice, who has had a religious conversion (is born again), and who is interested in leading others to the same kind of conversion experience.

Not too long ago, the movement of people with these convictions was thought to be dead, or at least on its last legs. But like a twentieth-century Lazarus, Evangelicalism is once again alive and well. The remarkable resurgence of Evangelicalism in the last two decades or so may be the most remarkable and noteworthy religious event in the United States in the twentieth century.

The evangelical renaissance is apparent in a number of ways. *Newsweek* magazine labeled 1976, the same year that self-professed evangelical Jimmy Carter won the presidency, "The Year of the Evangelical." Just four years later, the three major candidates in the 1980 presidential campaign—Jimmy Carter, Ronald Reagan, and John Anderson—were all self-professed evangelicals. *Time* magazine featured Jerry Falwell on one of its 1985 covers and devoted that issue's cover story to a generally favorable report about the new Fundamentalism that Falwell represents. Leading evangelicals appear on television talk-shows with increasing frequency.

But in spite of all the attention Evangelicalism is receiving from the media, the average American still knows relatively little about the movement. In fact, most of the forty to fifty million evangelicals in the United States would find it difficult to provide much in the way of systematic information about Evangelicalism.

A number of factors make it difficult to explain contemporary Evangelicalism in any short and simple package. For one thing, many people still think of the movement in terms of stereotypes that are no longer true and may, in fact, have never been true. For another thing, Evangelicalism is not a monolithic movement. No single leader or small group of leaders speaks for the entire movement. Evangelicalism is composed of a number of subcultures, each of which has additional subcultures.

Nowhere is the confusion and uncertainty about Evangelicalism more apparent than in America's mainline denominations. The word *mainline* is used to refer to "the large historical denominations having memberships reflecting great diversity, but leadership and official positions putting them generally in the liberal, ecumenically inclined and socially concerned wing of Christianity."[1] With some exceptions, America's so-called mainline denominations are those that belong to the National Council of Churches and that make up the American membership of the World Council of Churches. The list of mainline denominations usually includes The United Methodist Church, the United Presbyterian Church, The Episcopal Church, the United Church of Christ, the Lutheran Church in America, the American Lutheran Church,*

---

*In August of 1986, the American Lutheran Church and the Lutheran Church in America merged to form the Evangelical Lutheran Church in America.

the Disciples of Christ, American Baptist Churches, the Reformed Church in America, and similar but smaller denominations. Because the leadership of these denominations has tended to be more liberal and ecumenical than conservative, it used to be safe to contrast the mainline churches with Evangelicalism. But it is interesting to note that through much of the nineteenth century, these mainline denominations, or the earlier movements that merged to produce them, were themselves evangelical.

By all accounts, mainline Christianity in America has fallen on rather hard times. According to one representative of the mainline churches, "Mainline Protestantism today is in a serious state of disarray. These large, historic American denominations—liberal, ecumenical, and socially concerned, with their pluralistic membership and activist power establishments—are clearly in trouble."[2]

One sign of this trouble in the mainline churches is the steady decline of their constituencies for the past fifteen or so years. For example, between 1970 and 1977, The United Methodist Chuch lost almost 900,000 members. During the same period of time, United Presbyterians and the Episcopalians lost around a half-million members each. This significant decline in numbers has occurred across the spectrum of mainline denominations. But while the mainline churches have lost several million members, conservative churches have experienced a dramatic increase in their numbers. Naturally, as denominations lose hundreds of thousands of members, they also experience significant reductions in financial support. Consequently, mainline denominations have been forced to slash budgets, a move that has also required major decreases in the size of the denominational bureaucracy. While liberal theological seminaries that are often associated with mainline denominations are struggling to recruit students and even survive, evangelical seminaries are flourishing. Evangelical journals, such as *Christianity*

Today and *Eternity,* serve many more readers than the more mainline journals, such as *Christian Century.* Evangelical publishing houses are thriving as they produce a steady stream of quality academic books and more popular evangelical books that often sell hundreds of thousands of copies.

Mainline churches can no longer claim a monopoly on social activism. More likely than not, the group of religious people one might see picketing on behalf of one social cause or another will be composed largely of evangelicals. Evangelicals are no longer sitting by passively while the world goes by. They have become conscious of the social dimension of the gospel.

As if to add insult to injury, evangelicals are beginning to make moves to exercise a greater influence in several mainline denominations. Evangelicals are challenging the traditional power structure of denominations that thought a conservative presence was a thing of the past.

> Based in a massive parachurch movement (which is startling both in its range and its vigor) evangelicalism has already established itself as that part of the church which is growing, in contrast to the shrinking mainline. It has already, to a considerable extent, captured mainline youth, it is already dominating Protestant overseas mission work, and it has moved vigorously into the former liberal preserves of social and political action.[3]

The evangelical resurgence began outside the mainline churches. Fifty years ago, conservative Protestants had largely cut themselves off from the mainline denominations. Frustrated at having lost control of mainline institutions (schools, boards, and publications), they left those churches in droves and either joined smaller denominations that had remained untouched by the liberalism of the time or began new denominations. Anyone looking at a religious map of America in 1940 might have thought it safe to wager that Protestant conservatives would only continue to lose influence and power. No one in the mainline denominations was paying much attention to them. Conservatives had become isolated from what was judged to be the mainstream of American religious life and thought.

The evangelical resurgence started slowly after the end of World War II. Even after it began to pick up steam during the 1950s, most mainline leaders found it convenient to ignore Evangelicalism. Perhaps, they hoped, it would just go away. In important respects, the evangelical resurgence was connected with the national and international attention that evangelist Billy Graham began to receive because of his remarkably successful city-wide crusades in the 1950s. Another factor was the sometimes sputtering start that a small group of evangelical scholars made toward the publication of scholarly books and articles on subjects other than the Bible. This group included Carl F. H. Henry, Edward John Carnell, Gordon H. Clark, and Bernard Ramm. Still another factor was the 1956 founding of the evangelical journal *Christianity Today*.

It is now possible to look back and see that evangelical successes through most of the 1960s were most important because of the foundation that was being laid. Evangelicalism's real push to prominence on the national scene has occurred since 1970. One event that had a great deal to do with bringing evangelicals out of the closet was the 1973 *Roe v. Wade* Supreme Court decision. Conservative outrage over this decision to legalize abortion through the first six months of pregnancy did as much as anything to mobilize evangelicals. As the number of aborted fetuses passed one million a year, concerned Protestants found that they had natural allies in this cause among conservative Catholics and Jews.

Evangelicals also became alarmed over the increasing militancy of what they called Secular Humanism. Making what, in evangelical eyes, was a specious appeal to "the separation of church and state," humanists were in fact wedding their own brand of atheistic religion to the power of the state. Through their specious interpretation and illicit use of the First Amendment, secular humanists were seeking to exclude the religious beliefs and practices of the majority of Americans from public life while seeking the establishment of their own religion of Humanism. As a large body of Protestants, Catholics, and Jews argued, the so-called "establishment clause" must be interpreted in the light of what its authors intended it to mean. When this is done, the First Amendment does not outlaw prayer or the reading of the Bible in public facilities.

Modern technology also played a role in the evangelical resurgence. Conservative evangelists and Bible teachers had always used radio more effectively than had the mainline churches.* Evangelicals continued this advantage in their use of television. With varying degrees of competence and efficiency, a number of evangelical, fundamentalist, and pentecostal ministers began to develop nationwide television ministries. When even more advanced technology made it possible, an evangelical like Pat Robertson could build on the small network of television stations he had developed and his "700 Club" television show and develop a Christian Broadcasting Network (CBN) that could be beamed by satellite directly to cable systems across the country.

Evangelicals were also helped by the disarray in liberal theology and what can only be interpreted as a growing rejection of the liberalism that was a staple of so much mainline preaching. Evangelicals had something that many mainline churches seemed to have forgotten: the New Testament gospel. Evangelicals offered people a living God

---

*For the record, it should be noted that in the 1940s, liberal ecumenical churchmen preempted public service time for religion and opposed the sale of radio time to evangelicals.

who loved them and who wanted to deliver them from their sins. Evangelicalism offered people what the early church had to offer: a divine Christ who died for human sins and rose from the grave to demonstrate that salvation and eternal life are possible. This powerful message has always had the power to transform lives and societies.

Evangelicals are now estimated to number somewhere between forty and fifty million Americans. Of that number, as many as four or five million Roman Catholics regard themselves as evangelical. About half of America's Evangelicals live in the South and approximately half live outside of major metropolitan areas. Therefore, the percentage of evangelicals in cities like Dallas and Nashville will be considerably higher than the percentage in cities like New York, Chicago, Boston, and Cleveland. The percentage of evangelicals in smaller southern cities is greater than that in cities like Atlanta, Tampa, or Memphis. But the number of evangelicals in the North and in larger metropolitan areas continues to grow, largely due to the increased visibility of the evangelical message on television.

Not every mainline leader regards the evangelical resurgence as bad. Some admit that a renewed evangelical presence in their churches may help the mainline denominations recover some important things that have been lost or de-emphasized: concerns for doctrine, for Bible study, for spiritual living, and for evangelism. Some mainline leaders believe that the evangelical resurgence provides their churches with an opportunity for renewal. It may even make such churches truly pluralistic in the sense that even conservatives or traditionalists will once again be welcome and perhaps even given leadership roles.

CHAPTER TWO

Who Are the Evangelicals?

It may be impossible to appreciate the contemporary usage of *evangelical* if one fails to understand what the term has meant throughout the centuries. Just as the people called evangelicals have important ties to important Christian movements in earlier centuries, the word *evangelical* also has a history. An understanding of how the term was used in earlier centuries can help one recognize why it is such an appropriate label for today's evangelicals.

The word *evangelical* comes from the Greek word *euangelion*, which is the New Testament word for *gospel*. Literally, euangelion means "good news," a fitting term for the early Christians to use as their word for the gospel. The Christian gospel is, above all, God's good news to a lost and fallen world. The angel who announced the birth of Jesus said to the shepherds: "Do not be afraid. I bring you good news [*euangelion*] of great joy that will be for all the people" (Luke 2:10, NIV). That good news, of course, was word that the Savior, Christ the Lord, had been born in Bethlehem.

So far as we know, the church of the first century did not use "evangelical" as a name for any group of Christians, but it could have. In the context of the first century, an evangelical would simply have been someone who believed and shared the good news of the gospel.[1] Twentieth-century bearers of the label are evangelical in precisely this sense. They believe the gospel contained in the New Testament is true and they believe in sharing that good news with others.

After the Protestant Reformation in the sixteenth century, the word *evangelical* was used by certain groups of Protestants to distinguish themselves from Roman Catholics, who championed sacramental salvation. The Reformers were convinced that central elements of the first-century Christian message had been replaced by man-made doctrines. The Reformers believed that they had rediscovered the true gospel by going back to the original founding documents of the Christian faith: the New Testament. For such post-Reformation Christians, then, an evangelical was someone who had rediscovered the gospel of the early church.

During the eighteenth century, *evangelical* took on some additional nuances. The term was used to describe the great revivals or awakenings that swept first England and then the American colonies. Why were these periods of religious awakening called *evangelical* revivals? The answer lies in the fact that an evangelical is characterized not only by what he or she believes (the gospel), but also by how he or she lives, the scope of which was supposed to include the practice of evangelism. After the Reformation, people who had rediscovered the gospel were called evangelicals. During the eighteenth century, it was quite natural that the rediscovery of an evangelism similar to that practiced by the early church would be described by the word *evangelical*.

As evangelicals understand their movement, Evangelicalism is not a new phenomenon in the history of the Christian church. It did not begin in the twentieth century; Evangelicalism is rooted deeply in the history and beliefs of historic Christian orthodoxy. As evangelical Anglican James Packer puts it, "Evangelicalism is the oldest orthodoxy, grounded four-square upon the teaching of Christ and His apostles. . . . It stands in the direct line of Christian development in a way that other forms of the faith do not."[2] Evangelicalism, in other words, is simply historic Christian orthodoxy speaking to the theological, intellectual, moral, and social problems of the twentieth century.

Therefore, contemporary American evangelicals believe that their movement draws on a rich heritage. They share a commitment to the New Testament gospel and to the essential truths of that gospel that were rediscovered in the Reformation of the sixteenth century. They also share a commitment to the values that inspired the evangelical awakenings in the eighteenth and nineteenth centuries, revivals that among other things helped to bring into existence that group of Christians known as Methodists. It is important to remember that for more than a century after its beginnings in the awakenings of the eighteenth century early Methodism was an evangelical movement. Modern Evangelicalism's links to the past extend into the nineteenth century as well. Evangelical Protestantism remained the dominant force in American religious life until after the Civil War.[3] The new kid on the block, it would seem, is not evangelicalism but the various forms of liberalism that began to appear during the last century and a half.

The Evangelical Mosaic

Evangelicalism is anything but a monolithic movement. Because of its complexity, it has been compared to a ten-ring circus. Even though there are many different shows going on at the same time, the various parts fit together into a whole in ways that may not always be apparent at first glance. Dr. Timothy Smith of Johns Hopkins University has used the phrase "the evangelical mosaic" to illustrate the complexity of modern Evangelicalism. A mosaic, of course, is a picture or design that is composed of many smaller pieces. By itself, no one piece can begin to provide a picture of the whole. But as the pieces are gradually put together and one views the finished product from the proper distance, the completed picture becomes apparent. In order to obtain something that even approaches the whole picture of Evangelicalism, it is necessary to sort, arrange, and place the various pieces of the evangelical mosaic into their proper place in the whole. In the rest of this chapter, some of the most important pieces of the evangelical mosaic will be examined.

The Evangelical Subcultures

Evangelical professor Robert Webber states that Evangelicalism is "more than a particular historical movement or a listing of theological beliefs. It comprises a complex variety of subcultures within the larger evangelical culture."[4] Typically, three evangelical subcultures are distinguished: Fundamentalism, Pentecostalism, and what, for want of a better term, can be called the Evangelical Mainstream. Mainstream Evangelicalism is, itself, a complex movement that is difficult to define in few words. It includes all those evangelicals who, by their convictions, attitudes, and practices, fall somewhere in the center of the evangelical movement.

The relations among the three evangelical subcultures can be pictured in terms of three intersecting circles in which the center circle represents the Evangelical Mainstream. The fact that the circles representing Fundamentalism and Pentecostalism overlap the center circle illustrates two things. First, it is possible for an evangelical to exhibit some of the characteristics of a fundamentalist or pentecostal and still be part of the Evangelical Mainstream. Second, both Fundamentalism and Pentecostalism include people who are so extreme in one way or another that they belong outside the bounds of what can normally be regarded as Evangelicalism. Many fundamentalist extremists would object vehemently to being included within the evangelical camp. For such fundamentalists, Evangelicalism is synonymous with treason and embodies a betrayal of true Christianity. All of this means, then, that the precise relationship between Fundamentalism and Evangelicalism is very difficult to pin down; often, it must be settled on a person-by-person basis. A fundamentalist, like Jerry Falwell, may be regarded as a very conservative evangelical, while many fundamentalists associated with Bob Jones University are best viewed as part of a distinct religious group. A growing number of evangelicals are open to beliefs and practices that are pentecostal or charismatic. But a disturbingly large segment of the pentecostal movement holds views that are out of step with essential evangelical convictions. Some pentecostals, for example, are unitarians. Many extreme pentecostals elevate personal dreams and visions to the point where they have an authority equal to that of Scripture.

Later chapters in this book will examine Fundamentalism and Pentecostalism in greater detail. For now, it is enough to point out that fundamentalists, evangelicals, and most charismatics share a common commitment to an essential core of beliefs that includes the deity of Christ, the virgin birth, the incarnation, the substitutionary atonement, the bodily resurrection of Christ, and Christ's literal return to earth at the end of the age. Fundamentalists, evangelicals, and most charismatics share a high view of Scripture; they believe that the Bible is the Word of God and is normative for Christian belief and practice.

Mainstream evangelicals, fundamentalists, and charismatics naturally disagree about many things. Charismatics complain that other evangelicals and fundamentalists ignore and even deny an important second work of grace, the baptism of the Holy Spirit, that is necessary to empower the Christian for service and holy living. Non-charismatics worry that pentecostals put the cart of subjective religious experience before the horse, which in their analogy means the written Word of God, the ultimate test of religious experience. More extreme fundamentalists accuse evangelicals of compromising with unbelievers, of placing too much emphasis upon education, of allowing liberal attitudes toward the Bible, and of losing their evangelistic fervor. While acknowledging that such fundamentalist charges have force in some cases, mainstream evangelicals complain that the extreme fundamentalists are still prone to anti-intellectualism, theological nit-picking, and bitterness of spirit. It is clear that Evangelicalism is not one big happy family.

But both mainstream evangelicals and fundamentalists deplore the theological fuzziness that seems to prevail in many of America's mainline churches and their educational institutions. Both mainstream evangelicals and fundamentalists object when religious groups (like certain pentecostals) exalt subjective religious experience at the expense of sound doctrine and the clear teaching of Scripture. The major theme that runs through all three evangelical subcultures is the necessity of personal salvation. All three groups hold that conversion is a definite, decisive, and profoundly life-changing experience.[5]

Mainstream evangelicals, fundamentalists and evangelical charismatics differ from religious liberalism in their persuasion that doctrine is an essential ingredient of the Christian faith. Men and women gain God's new life by believing the gospel. Evangelicals disagree with theological liberals who often appear to suggest that the content of a person's belief is irrelevant or unimportant to his or her relationship to God.

Evangelicalism and the Denominations

Evangelicalism is not a denomination in the traditional sense. It may be best to think of Evangelicalism as a transdenominational movement in the sense that it transcends traditional denominational boundaries. Nevertheless, the relationship of Evangelicalism to America's mainline churches and to smaller, but more evangelical, denominations is necessary if the complete picture is to be seen.

The Mainline Denominations

As noted earlier, evangelicals are making a strong comeback in the older, established mainline denominations. These denominations are in fact committed by their historic confessions or creeds to evangelical doctrine, although seminaries and pastors today tend to neglect this tradition or view it critically. Several of these denominations have organized groups of evangelical pastors and laypeople; one example of such a group is the "Good News" movement within The United Methodist Church. In some cases, these mainline evangelicals object to denominational support for operations of the National Council and World Council of Churches that aid what they regard as radical and subchristian causes. They attempt to offer a conservative alternative within their denomination. One of the ways in which these mainline evangelicals express their discontent is through the offering plate. Why, they ask, should they continue to pay the bills to support individuals and institutions that undermine what they believe is essential to Christianity?

More Distinctively Evangelical Denominations

Most evangelicals belong to smaller, non-mainline denominations that are predominantly or entirely evangelical. Some of these evangelical denominations were originally ethnic or immigrant churches that were left relatively untouched by the rise of Protestant liberalism earlier in this century; both the Baptist General Conference and the Evangelical Free Church illustrate denominations like this. Many evangelical denominations broke away from older denominations; for example, the Free Methodist Church began because of a dispute over slavery. The Conservative Baptist Association and the more fundamentalist General Association of Regular Baptists began as a result of theological liberalism in the Northern Baptist Convention (now known as American Baptist Churches). The Orthodox Presbyterian Church resulted from a similar theological dispute within the Northern Presbyterian Church. Other evangelical denominations began as a result of a desire to meet an important need that was going unmet; an example here would be the Christian and Missionary Alliance. Often, evangelical denominations have sprung up in response to a perceived need to stress a particular doctrine or set of doctrines, for example, the several denominations that stress the pentecostal experience.

The three evangelical subcultures are well-represented by the various evangelical denominations. The largest of the pentecostal denominations is the Assemblies of God, which is also one of the fastest growing churches in the United States. The fundamentalist subculture is represented by the Baptist Bible Fellowship (Jerry Falwell's fellowship)* and the General Association of Regular Baptists Churches. In addition to some of the denominations mentioned earlier, other mainstream evangelical denominations include the Presbyterian Church in America, the Reformed Episcopal Church, the Wesleyan Church, the Church of the Nazarene, the Churches of Christ, and several dozen more. Anyone familiar with more than a few of these denominations can quickly recognize the diversity of evangelical belief and practice.

Several denominations—such as the Christian Reformed Church, the Southern Baptist Convention, and in some respects even the Lutheran Church-Missouri Synod—do not fit very neatly into the categories provided earlier. To some extent, ambivalence about such denominations is due to a

---

*Interestingly, some segments of the Baptist Bible Fellowship oppose Falwell, because he is insufficiently fundamentalist in their view.

greater variety of theological convictions than one finds in a more typically evangelical denomination. The Southern Baptist Convention, with its fourteen million members, is difficult to classify. Without question, the vast majority of Southern Baptist laypeople are conservative in their beliefs; many of them would qualify as fundamentalists. A growing number of conservative Southern Baptist pastors, however, have charged that Southern Baptist educational institutions and agencies have come under the control of liberals. For several years, the Convention's annual meeting has been the battleground for a struggle between opposing forces within the Convention. Every year since 1979, the more conservative wing of the Southern Baptists has managed to elect its candidate over what has been described as more liberal candidates. Considering the rules by which Southern Baptists govern themselves, this annual election is crucial since the Convention president appoints committees that, in turn, appoint the people who serve on the boards governing Southern Baptist seminaries. Once a sufficient number of conservatives are appointed to these boards, Southern Baptist evangelicals believe, they stand a better chance of saving their seminaries and their convention from the kind of liberalism that gained control of northern mainline denominations earlier in the century. Efforts are presently underway that many hope will bring a peaceful resolution to the struggle. But some observers believe that it is only a matter of time before some kind of major split occurs.

Parachurch Organizations

Perhaps nowhere is Evangelicalism's transdenominational character more apparent than in its many parachurch organizations. Parachurch organizations transcend traditional denominational boundaries in the pursuit of specific Christian objectives. They function outside of any denominational controls.

While evangelical parachurch organizations may technically include many television ministries (the electronic church) and evangelical journals and publishing houses, this section of the chapter will focus on six organizations that minister to young people in high school, in college, and in the military: Campus Crusade for Christ, Inter-Varsity Christian Fellowship, Young Life, Youth for Christ, Navigators, and the Fellowship of Christian Athletes.

Founded by Bill Bright in 1951, Campus Crusade for Christ is the largest and most aggressively evangelistic of the evangelical parachurch organizations. Headquartered in Arrowhead Springs, California, the sixty-five hundred staff members of Campus Crusade minister in more than eighty countries. Originally designed as an evangelistic ministry to college students, Campus Crusade now includes ministries to high school students, to young people in the military, to Christian athletes, and to international students studying in the United States. It also carries on a prison ministry.

Inter-Varsity Christian Fellowship is an American outgrowth of a movement that began in England during the nineteenth century. Presently operating on more than eight hundred college campuses, Inter-Varsity differs from Campus Crusade by being somewhat more low-key in its evangelistic effort and by stressing an intellectual dimension in its presentation of the gospel. Inter-Varsity carries on an extensive publishing ministry through Inter-Varsity Press and its journal, *His* magazine. A small branch of the Inter-Varsity organization, Theological Students Fellowship, maintains an evangelical witness on the campuses of non-evangelical seminaries. Every three years, Inter-Varsity holds a huge missionary convention at the University of Illinois in Urbana. As many as eighteen thousand college students attend these conferences to hear internationally known evangelicals like

31

Billy Graham. Evangelicals give Urbana much of the credit for the continuing vitality of evangelical missions.

Young Life and Youth for Christ work primarily with high school students. Young Life was started in 1941. Now headquartered in Colorado Springs, Colorado, it is active in more than one thousand high schools. Founded in 1944, Youth for Christ adopted a different method of operation by emphasizing large weekly youth rallies that were full of features designed to catch the interest and attention of teenagers. Billy Graham's first opportunities to address large audiences came during his work as a Youth for Christ evangelist during the 1940s. Approximately one thousand Youth for Christ staff members help run Youth for Christ clubs in more than one thousand American high schools.

The Navigators got their name from their beginnings as a ministry to enlisted men in the Navy during World War II. The organization now works with young people in all branches of the military through evangelism and Bible study that encourages Christian growth. The organization has expanded its outreach to include college campuses and maintains a vigorous publishing ministry.

Aware of the influence that respected athletes can have on people of all ages, the Fellowship of Christian Athletes seeks to evangelize amateur and professional athletes, to help them grow as Christians, and to encourage them to use their testimony to influence other athletes as well as high school and college students. The Fellowship presently has more than fifty thousand members.

The Electronic Church

If Evangelicalism reaches thousands of young people through its parachurch organizations, it presents the gospel weekly to millions of adults through what has become known as "the electronic church." America now has over thirteen hundred radio stations and about twenty-five television stations that broadcast predominantly or exclusively religious programming. There are four Christian cable television networks: the Christian Broadcasting Network (received in thirty million homes), the PTL Network (in around thirteen million households), a Southern Baptist cable network (about one and a half million homes), and Jerry Falwell's new Liberty Broadcasting Network. Falwell's network began with cable access to approximately two million homes, but hopes, within two or three years, to have thirty million subscribers. In addition, Jerry Falwell ("The Old-Time Gospel Hour"), D. James Kennedy, and Robert Schuller ("The Hour of Power") are just three examples of evangelicals whose different approaches and messages are carried by television to every corner of the nation. Billy Graham offers several hour-long television programs each year that are taped from his city-wide crusades.

According to a 1984 University of Pennsylvania survey, approximately thirteen million people watch religious television programs on a regular basis. *Time* magazine (Feb. 17, 1986) cited a Nielsen survey that shows that when cable subscribers are counted, about 40 percent of America's families watch Christian television programs at least once a month. At least once a month, twenty-seven million Americans watch segments of Pat Robertson's "700 Club." Evangelical access to almost every home in America in this way will continue to be an important factor in the continuing expansion of evangelical influence.

Evangelical Missions

Overseas missionary activity by representatives of mainline denominations has been decreasing. Between 1969 and 1975, the number of foreign missionaries working with mainline churches dropped from eight thousand to some five thousand.[6]

The number is even lower today. Evangelicals have an explanation for this decline in mainline missions. When a denomination deemphasizes evangelism and the historic Christian message, there is less incentive for people brought up under that kind of ministry to undertake the sacrifices required for missionary activity.

The evangelical message and its emphasis on evangelism leads naturally to a recognition of the abiding relevance of Christ's Great Commission: "Therefore go and make disciples of all nations, baptizing them in the name of the Father and of the Son and of the Holy Spirit, and teaching them to obey everything I have commanded you" (Matthew 28:19-20). Evangelical missions have become much more sophisticated in its dealing with people who belong to different cultures. While conservative missionaries in the past often lacked training in areas other than the Bible, the evangelical missionary of today has frequently had several years of graduate study. Because of the obvious importance of the Bible, evangelicals are giving much attention to the translation of the Bible into languages in which no Bible is presently available. Because the people who use these languages are often illiterate, Bible-translators must spend years reducing a language to writing, then translating the Bible into that language, and finally teaching the illiterate members of the tribe to read. The organization known as Wycliff Bible Translators has been a pioneer in this kind of missionary work.

Evangelical Publishing

Major evangelical publishers include Zondervan Publishing House, Word Books, Tyndale House, Crossway Books, Thomas Nelson, Multnomah Books, Fleming H. Revell, Inter-Varsity Press, and Baker Book House. Eerdmans Publishing Company has begun to issue a growing number of non-evangelical books, but is still regarded by many as an evangelical publisher. A number of non-evangelical companies, such as Harper and Row and John Knox Press, publish books by evangelical authors. In addition, the work of evangelical scholars shows up regularly in the listings of such academic presses as Oxford University Press and the University of Notre Dame Press.

Even when evangelical books sell hundreds of thousands of copies, they seldom appear in the best-seller lists, since such lists are compiled on the basis of sales in selected secular bookstores. The lists ignore the more than thirty-five hundred bookstores that belong to the Christian Booksellers Association. While the CBA has no doctrinal requirements for membership, its constituency is predominantly evangelical. Annual gross sales for bookstores associated with the CBA approach two hundred million dollars.

Popular evangelical authors whose books regularly sell more than one hundred thousand copies include Billy Graham, Robert Schuller, Francis Schaeffer, James Dobson, Richard Foster, Charles Swindoll, Tim LaHaye, Charles Colson, and Pat Robertson. While there has been a significant increase in the quantity and quality of scholarly academic books by evangelicals, the evangelical public concentrates its book purchases on lighter fare. Other than the Bible, the best-selling book of the 1970s was a dispensational interpretation of Bible prophecy by Hal Lindsey entitled *The Late Great Planet Earth*. For many informed evangelicals, Lindsey's book was living proof that the sales of a book have little in common with the quality of that book.

Evangelical publishing includes more than books. Several companies—such as Scripture Press, Gospel Light, and David C. Cook—publish enormously popular materials for Sunday schools and Vacation Bible Schools. The evangelical cause is helped considerably by the existence of a number of quality magazines and journals. Near the top of many lists is *Christianity Today*, a bimonthly magazine that is read by several hundred thousand people. During its early years after its founding in 1956, *Christianity Today* did much to acquaint its readers with the evangelical stand on important issues. The magazine has reduced its scholarly content considerably in recent years and often appears over-anxious to appease various evangelical factions on especially touchy issues. *Eternity*, a smaller evangelical magazine published out of offices in Philadelphia, attempted briefly in the mid-1980s to raise the intellectual level of evangelical journalism. A recent change of its staff will undoubtedly lead *Eternity* in some new directions.

Other successful evangelical monthlies directed at more popular audiences include *Moody Monthly*, *Christian Life*, and *Christian Herald*. Inter-Varsity Christian Fellowship publishes *His* magazine, targeted at college students. *The Fundamentalist Journal*, published by people associated with Jerry Falwell's "Old Time Gospel Hour," is slowly evolving into an attractive and respectable spokesjournal for the evangelical right. The views of more liberal evangelicals can be found in *The Reformed Journal*, which has ties to Eerdmans Publishing Company, to Calvin College, and to segments of the Christian Reformed Church.

People hungry for social and political radicalism can find it in *Sojourners*, a well-designed and articulate journal often criticized for placing its political ideology ahead of the gospel.[7] Another journal, *The Other Side*, represents a similar kind of left-wing Evangelicalism.

It is obvious that evangelicals believe in the power of the printed word. There is no shortage of well-run organizations to disseminate evangelical publications. The major weakness is the difficulty of getting the evangelical public to read the more serious literature that will help it become acquainted with important intellectual issues.

Evangelical Colleges and Seminaries

The growth of Evangelicalism has been helped in no small part by a network of evangelical colleges and seminaries spread out across the country. These schools cover the spectrum of evangelical opinion. Many of them have become excellent and fully accredited institutions, with well-trained faculty holding doctorates from respected universities.

Not surprisingly, many evangelical colleges and seminaries are affiliated with and supported by evangelical denominations. Examples of such schools include Calvin College (The Christian Reformed Church), Bethel College and Seminary (Baptist General Conference), Trinity College and Trinity Evangelical Divinity School (The Evangelical Free Church), Houghton College and Marion College (The Wesleyan Church), Roberts Wesleyan College and Seattle-Pacific University (The Free Methodist Church), King College (Presbyterian), Covenant College and Covenant Theological Seminary (Presbyterian Church in America), Conservative Baptist Seminary (Conservative Baptist Association), North Park College and Theological Seminary (Evangelical Covenant), and Asbury College and Asbury Theological Seminary (not officially related to The United Methodist Church, but strongly Methodist in orientation).

Many evangelical colleges and some seminaries are non-denominational. A list of these would include Wheaton College, Gordon College and Gordon-Conwell Theological Seminary, Biola University, Taylor University, Westmont College, Fuller Theological Seminary, Dallas Theological Seminary, Reformed Theological Seminary, and Westminster Theological Seminary. At a time when enrollment in non-evangelical seminaries continues to decline, evangelical seminaries are flourishing. Fuller Theological Seminary now reports an enrollment of twenty-five hundred. Dallas Seminary and

Trinity Evangelical Divinity School both have enrollments of around one thousand.

The largest and fastest growing evangelical college is Jerry Falwell's Liberty University (formerly Liberty Baptist College) in Lynchburg, Virginia. Liberty University now enrolls more than seven thousand students and is regionally accredited. The university includes a seminary (Liberty Baptist Theological Seminary) and plans to begin offering doctoral programs in a few years.

The fundamentalist wing of Evangelicalism is represented by such schools as Bob Jones University, Tennessee Temple College, Baptist Bible Collge, Grand Rapids Baptist College, Cedarville College, and many others. While some of these schools, like Cedarville, are regionally accredited, others, like Bob Jones University, refuse even to seek accreditation on the ground that it would require them to compromise important convictions.

Pentecostal higher education is more closely aligned with such denominational colleges as Evangel College (Assemblies of God), Lee College (Church of God, Cleveland, Tennessee), and Oral Roberts University. CBN University, associated with Pat Robertson's CBN television network, offers work exclusively at the graduate level.

Other Evangelical Organizations

Two other evangelical organizations deserve mention. Founded in 1942, the National Association of Evangelicals represents a number of evangelical interests and provides them with a voice at the national level. Most of the smaller evangelical denominations belong to or work closely with the NAE. In addition, single churches or small associations of churches and even individual persons may join the organization. Its purpose is to represent "all evangelical believers in all denominations and groups."

The Evangelical Theological Society, founded in 1949, serves as a rallying point for evangelical professors of Bible, theology, and related areas. With a regular membership of one thousand, the society annually holds one national meeting, several regional meetings, and publishes a quarterly, *The Journal of the Evangelical Theological Society*, that is geared to the interests of its membership. Members of the ETS must hold at least one graduate degree in religion and sign a very brief doctrinal statement attesting their belief in the inerrancy of the Bible. The society does not speak exclusively for evangelical scholars, since many who could sign the doctrinal statement decline to join the organization.

Conclusion

This chapter began by comparing Evangelicalism to a ten-ring circus. The brief overview of Evangelicalism in this chapter may suggest that the analogy of a ten-ring circus is far too conservative. No overarching bureaucracy holds this diversity of people and opinions together. No single leader, or group of leaders, speaks for all or even a portion of evangelicals. What evangelicals have in common is a set of beliefs and a set of causes that grow out of those beliefs. While they differ about a number of doctrines, about church polity, about forms of worship, about the mode of baptism, and about how they view the Christian's responsibility to society, they agree about the utter importance of the New Testament gospel. They agree about the essential components of that gospel, and they agree on the ultimate authority of the Bible and that they have a responsibility to share the truth of the Christian message with the world. Who are the evangelicals? No short and simple answer to that question can be given. But at least a start toward finding an answer has been made.

CHAPTER THREE

Evangelical Roots

This chapter will examine three important links between contemporary Evangelicalism and important events or developments in the history of Christianity: the early Christian consensus, reflected in the first creeds of the church; the attempt by Protestant Reformers to set the Christian ship back on course; and the effects of the various periods of revival upon the church in the eighteenth and nineteenth centuries.

Orthodox Christianity

The first step that must be taken by anyone who wishes to understand Evangelicalism is to recognize its ties to the set of essential beliefs that all orthodox Christians—Roman Catholic, Eastern Orthodox, and Protestant—share. To a large extent, this Catholic-Protestant consensus is reflected in such early Christian statements as the Nicene Creed and the Apostles' Creed. This consensus is referred to in several ways. It can be called historic or traditional Christian theism. Often it is simply called orthodoxy. According to theologian William Hordern, "Orthodox Christianity is that form of Christianity which won the support of the overwhelming majority of Christians and which is expressed by most of the official proclamations or creeds of Christian groups."[1]

The basic core of evangelical belief is neither new nor unique to Evangelicalism. When evangelicals affirm their belief in the deity of Jesus Christ or in the bodily resurrection of Christ, they are aligning themselves with historic Christian orthodoxy. The essence of that orthodoxy can be summarized in ten basic beliefs.

1. Theism

The Apostles' Creed begins with the words, "I believe in God the Father Almighty, maker of heaven and earth. . . ." These words express the essence of theism, which is the belief in one supremely powerful, personal God, who created the heavens and the earth. Theism differs from polytheism in its affirmation that there is only one God (Deuteronomy 6:4). It parts company with the various forms of pantheism by insisting that God is personal and must not be confused with the world that is his creation. Theism must also be distinguished from panentheism, the increasingly popular position that regards the world as an eternal being that God needs in much the same way a human soul needs a body. Theists also reject panentheistic attempts to limit God's power and knowledge, which have the effect of making the God of panentheism a finite being.[2]

Evangelicals are theists, then, who believe that God is one, is a spirit, is personal, and is the almighty and omniscient creator. While Christian theists believe many other things about God (for example, God is love), the divine attributes noted in this section make up the essential feature of theism.

2. The Trinity

Historic Christian theism is trinitarian. To quote the Apostles' Creed once more: "I believe in God the Father Almighty . . . and in Jesus Christ his only Son our Lord . . . [and] in the Holy Spirit." The language of the Nicene Creed is similar: "I believe in one God: the Father Almighty . . . and in one Lord Jesus Christ . . . and I believe in the Holy Ghost. . . ."

The doctrine of the trinity reflects the Christian conviction that the Father, the Son, and the Holy Spirit are three distinct centers of consciousness that share fully in the one divine nature and in the activities of the other persons of the trinity. The doctrine is a natural outgrowth of the church's efforts to reconcile those biblical passages that teach that there is but one God (Deuteronomy 6:4) with other texts that identify three distinct persons as God (Matthew 3:16; John 14:16, 17; II Corinthians 13:14; Ephesians 4:4-6). The triune nature of the Christian God is illustrated in Jesus' Great Commission, in which he commanded his disciples to go and make disciples from all nations and then baptize them in the *one* name of the Father, Son, and Holy Spirit (Matthew 28:19).

3. *The Deity of Jesus Christ*

In the words of the Nicene Creed,[3] Christians believe "in one Lord Jesus Christ, the only begotten Son of God: begotten of the Father before all worlds, God of God, Light of Light, very God of very God, begotten, not made, being of one substance with the Father." Like all orthodox Christians, evangelicals believe that Jesus was not simply a human being. Nor is it correct to say that Jesus was Godlike. Orthodox Christians believe that Jesus Christ is God.[4] As British evangelical John Stott explains: "Jesus was the Son of God. We shall not be satisfied with a verdict declaring his vague divinity; it is his deity which we mean to establish. We believe him to possess an eternal and essential relation to God possessed by no other person. We regard him neither as God in human disguise, nor as a man with divine qualities, but as the God-man."[5]

The essence of this view of Jesus is expressed in the first chapter of the fourth Gospel, which teaches:

> In the beginning was the Word, and the Word was with God, and the Word was God. He was with God in the beginning. Through

him [the Word] all things were made; without him nothing was made that has been made. . . . The Word became flesh and made his dwelling among us. We have seen his glory, the glory of the one and only Son, who came from the Father, full of grace and truth. (John 1:1-3, 14)[6]

4. The Incarnation

Christians use the word "incarnation" to express their belief that the birth of Jesus Christ marked the entrance of the eternal and divine Son of God into the human race. Evangelicals believe in the virgin birth of Christ (Matthew 1:18, 25) as earnestly as do traditional Roman Catholics. Jesus was as much a human being as any man or woman, although he was without sin. But Jesus was also fully God.

5. The Atonement

Jesus entered this world expressly to die. The purpose of his death was to make things right between the Holy God and sinful humans who, because of sin, are separated from God. Jesus' death was neither an accident nor an act of martyrdom. He died as a sacrifice for human sins; he died as the fulfillment of all that the Old Testament system of sacrifice foreshadowed.[7]

This is the inescapable message of the New Testament. When Paul explained what he meant by the Christian gospel, he summarized the gospel in two points: "Christ died for our sins . . . and was raised again the third day according to the Scriptures" (I Corinthians 15:3-4). In Romans, Paul wrote: "Christ died for the ungodly. . . . While we were still sinners, Christ died for us" (Romans 5:6, 8). As John Stott summarizes this important truth:

> No religious observances or good deeds of ours could ever earn our forgiveness. . . . [Christ] died to atone for our sins for the

simple reason that we cannot atone for them ourselves. If we could, his atoning death would be redundant. Indeed, to claim that we can secure God's favour by our own efforts is an insult to Jesus Christ. For it is tantamount to saying that we can manage without him; he really need not have bothered to die.[8]

It is important, evangelicals insist, that human beings come to realize that Christ died for each one of us. He took the punishment that every human being deserves. He died in our place. And because he bore the penalty for our sin in his body, it is possible for all who believe in him to be pardoned, forgiven, justified, and reconciled to God. In Paul's words, "When we were God's enemies, we were reconciled to him through the death of his Son" (Romans 5:10).

6. *The Resurrection*

The resurrection of Christ is the central event of the New Testament. The apostle Paul made belief in the resurrection one of two conditions that had to be met before any person could be considered a genuine Christian.[9] It was Paul's own encounter with the risen Christ that transformed him from an enemy of Christianity and a persecutor of Christians into the faith's greatest missionary and theologian.

In some parts of Christendom, it has become fashionable to attempt to explain away the miracle of Christ's resurrection. In one such view, Jesus simply continued to live in the hearts of his followers. Such a theory, however, is totally out of step with historic Christianity, which insists that Christ did rise from the dead. The tomb was empty; the risen Christ appeared to his disciples on numerous occasions.[10]

Paul made it clear that if the resurrection of Jesus had never happened, Christians could have no hope. "And if Christ has not been raised, your faith is futile; you are still in your sins. Then those also who have fallen asleep in Christ are lost. If only for this life we have hope in Christ, we are to be pitied more than all men" (I Corinthians 15:17-19). Paul regarded the resurrection as a historical event, supported by the strongest possible eyewitness testimony (I Corinthians 15:5-8). For Paul, the historicity of the resurrection was a necessary condition for the truth of Christianity and for the validity of Christian belief (I Corinthians 15:12-19). Evangelicals join with other orthodox Christians in sharing this conviction.

7. Human Sin

John Stott explains the importance of the unpopular subject of sin: "So we turn from Christ to man, from the sinlessness and glory that are in him to the sin and shame that are in us. Only then, after we have clearly grasped what we are, shall we be in a position to perceive the wonder of what he has done for us and offers to us. Only when we have had our malady accurately diagnosed shall we be willing to take the medicine prescribed."[11]

Christianity simply will not make sense to people who fail to understand and appreciate the Christian doctrine of sin. Every human being lives in a condition of sin and alienation from his or her creator. Each has sinned and fallen short of God's standard (Romans 3:23). This standard of God's righteousness, Paul makes clear, is Jesus Christ himself (Romans 3:21–4:25). As Stott counsels, sin "is not a convenient invention of parsons to keep them in their job; it is a fact of human experience."[12] This sin that separates us from God and enslaves us "is more than an unfortunate outward act or habit; it is a deep-seated inward corruption. In fact, the sins we commit are merely outward and visible manifestations of this inward and invisible malady, the symptoms of a moral disease. . . . Because sin is an inward corruption of human nature we are in bondage. It is not so much certain acts or habits which enslave us, but rather the evil infection from which these spring."[13] The reason human beings commit acts of sin is that they are infected by a sinful human nature.

8. Conversion and Redemption

Orthodoxy recognizes the human need for forgiveness and redemption and stresses that the blessings of salvation are possible because of Jesus' death and resurrection. The New Testament uses the word *redemption* to refer to the fact that humans are in bondage to sin and can only be set free by God's power in Christ. One of the most important New Testament words dealing with salvation is *justification,* which British evangelical James Packer explains as "forgiveness *plus.*" Justification, Packer declares,

> signifies not only washing out of the past, but also acceptance and the gift of a righteous man's status for the future. Also, justification is final, being a decision on which God will never go back, and so it is the basis of assurance, whereas present forgiveness does not necessarily argue more than temporary forbearance. So justification—public acquittal and reinstatement before God's judgment-seat—is actually the richer concept.[14]

The notion of conversion carries with it the idea of radical change. Evangelicals note the importance that Jesus placed upon conversion when he said: "I tell you the truth, unless you change [are converted] and become like little children, you will never enter the kingdom of heaven" (Matthew 18:3). Christ's redemptive work, evangelicals believe, is the ground or basis of human salvation. But human beings are required to repent (be sorry) of their sins and believe. Accepting Christ as one's Lord and Savior brings about a new birth, a new heart, a new relation to God, and a new power to live (John 3:3-21; Hebrews 8:10-12; I John 3:1-2; and Galatians 2:20). In Paul's words,

"Therefore, if anyone is in Christ, he is a new creation; the old has gone, the new has come!" (II Corinthians 5:17).

9. The Christian Life

Christian conversion does not suddenly make the new Christian perfect. But the Christian has God's nature and God's Spirit within and is called to live a particular kind of life in obedience to God's will. Once the Christian life begins in the divine act of justification, it must be nurtured through a process that the New Testament calls *sanctification* (Romans 8). Christians are to grow in holiness. But the good works that God expects to see in the life of the believer are not something that the believer can do through his or her own effort. The New Testament makes it clear that the moral deeds and character that God desires to see are fruits of God's Spirit. They are made possible by the power of God in the believer (Galatians 2:20; 5:22-23).

10. The Final Judgment

The Apostles' Creed states that Christ shall come from heaven "to judge the quick [living] and the dead." There has always been an important future dimension to the Christian's life and faith. Christians look back to the finished work of Jesus Christ that is the ground of their salvation and of their present Christian life. But they also, in the words of the Nicene Creed, "look for the resurrection of the dead, and the life of the world to come." At the end of the age, Christ will come to earth a second time and will judge all human beings (Matthew 25:31-46; 13:24-29, 36-43).

Orthodox Christians have differed greatly over many of the details connected with the end times and about the chronological order in which the events will occur. But they do agree about the following: (1) God will bring human history to a close in his way and at his time; (2) Christ will return a second time in power and glory; (3) all human beings will be judged; (4) believers and unbelievers will be separated for eternity; and (5) believers will never again know death, pain, sorrow, or suffering (Revelation 19:11–21:4).

Summary

The first part of this chapter has noted ten basic areas of belief about which traditional Catholics and Protestants agree. The substance of this Catholic-Protestant consensus appears in the early creeds of the church, which have their own warrant in the teaching of Scripture. With regard to specific details of some of these beliefs (such as justification and the relationship between faith and works), evangelicals and Catholics have, at least in the past, parted company. In the next section of this chapter, disagreements between evangelical Protestants and Catholics will become relevant.

The Reformation

The Protestant Reformers reaffirmed all of the traditional tenets of Christian orthodoxy, including the trinity, the deity of Christ, the virgin birth, and the bodily resurrection of Christ. Their goal was to call the church back to other important Christian convictions that had become lost, ignored, or abandoned during the Middle Ages. They also challenged a number of beliefs, added during the Middle Ages, that conflicted with the New Testament.

One of the important doctrines recovered by the Reformers was justification by faith. The Reformers objected to the Roman Catholic practice that encouraged its members to seek ways of building up their own personal righteousness through good deeds and acts of penance. James Packer summarizes this disagreement:

> In the past (things are less clear-cut today) Roman Catholics did not grasp the decisiveness of present justification, nor see that Christ's righteousness . . . is its whole ground, nor realize that our part is to stop trying to earn it, and simply take it as God's free gift of grace. So they insisted that sacraments, "good works," and purgatorial pains hereafter were all necessary means of final acceptance, because they were among the grounds on which that acceptance was based. But the Reformers preached, as Paul did, full and final acceptance through a decisive act of forgiveness here and now; this, they said, is by faith alone.[15]

As the Augsburg Confession of 1530 put it, "Men cannot be justified in God's sight by their own strengths, merits, or works; on the contrary, they are justified freely on account of Christ through faith, when they believe that they are received into grace and that their sins are remitted on account of Christ who by his own death made satisfaction for our sins. This faith God imputes for righteousness in his own sight" (Article 4).

One reason the church had lost sight of the purity of the New Testament's teaching about justification by faith alone was that it had diluted the authority of the Bible by adding a parallel authority—church tradition. The Reformers recognized that the appeal to tradition was being used to subvert other important elements of traditional Christianity. Whenever the church of that time wavered on important beliefs or began to substitute new beliefs, the changes were justified not by appeals to Scripture (the clear sense of which contradicted the changes), but by appeals to tradition. And so the Reformers also broke with the Catholic Church in their belief that the Scriptures alone are the Christian's ultimate rule of faith and practice. They rejected tradition as a religious authority equal or superior to Scripture. They gave the Bible primacy over human experience and human teaching, including the teaching of church leaders, church councils, and even the pope. For the Reformers, the Christian church has only one ultimate authority—the Bible. This is not to say that Protestants should ignore the traditions of the church, but such traditions can never stand on the same level as Scripture. Tradition, such as the teachings of the Reformers, must always be tested by the written Word of God.

Other Protestant differences with Roman Catholicism followed from their commitment to the principle of *Sola Scriptura*. Many of these disagreements were included in the important Protestant confessions formulated in the century following the Reformation. But the basic core of these confessions continued to be the orthodox consensus noted earlier in this chapter.

The Evangelical Revivals

The Reformation was a needed corrective for what the Reformers saw as errors that had crept into Roman Catholic doctrine and practice. Unfortunately, those who followed the Reformers soon fell into their own errors. Protestantism in many places became characterized by a cold, dead orthodoxy sometimes called Protestant scholasticism. This Protestant scholasticism tended to encase the religious convictions of the Reformation only in the hard shell of creeds, assent to which was often made to appear more important than conversion and the inward life of the Spirit. There was a definite need for religious revivals to call people to decision, commitment, and conversion and that would once again stir up the fires of religious enthusiasm. Even in the American colonies, a marked decline in religious zeal could be seen. America entered a stage of religious sluggishness that paralleled the decline of spirituality in England and on the European continent. Western Christianity was in need of a second Reformation. But what was needed this time was a Reformation not so much of doctrine as one of spiritual life.

Contemporary Evangelicalism owes much to developments within Protestantism after the Reformation. One such development was the religious awakenings that took place in the eighteenth century. These awakenings took different forms and were called by different names, depending on where they occurred. In Germany, the evangelical revival took the form of Pietism, which had a profound influence on the Lutheran tradition. Pietism stressed the new birth and the new life that was supposed to follow conversion. The most significant thing to come out of the eighteenth century evangelical revival in England was the Methodist movement, led by John Wesley (1703–1758) and his brother Charles (1707–1788).

America experienced several waves of revival. The first Great Awakening in America took place around 1740. Two of its early leaders were Presbyterians Theodore Frelinghuysen (1691–1747) and Gilbert Tennent (1703–1764). Central to their message was the evangelical call for men and women to repent of their sins and believe the gospel. An important leader of this awakening in New England was Jonathan Edwards (1703–1758). The preaching of Englishman George Whitefield (1714–1770), an early associate of John Wesley, was also instrumental.

America's second Great Awakening started in the 1790s and continued into the nineteenth century. Its subsequent effect on evangelical belief and practice would surpass that of the revivals fifty years before. The Second Awakening was centered in two places—in New England and on the frontier, especially in Kentucky and Tennessee.

Even though Methodism did not reach the American colonies until 1771 (in the person of Francis Asbury), by 1850 it had become the largest Christian body in America.[16]

Throughout the nineteenth century, American Evangelicalism was profoundly affected by this growing Methodist presence. Wesley's Arminian theology and its emphasis on free will offered a distinct counterpoint to the Calvinistic or Reformed theology that had dominated religious thinking in America before 1800. American Methodism also produced a large body of Christians who became interested in personal holiness. Wesleyanism taught that Christians should seek sanctification as zealously as they had pursued justification.

> Methodists in the nineteenth century never lost a feeling for the necessity of initial conversion to Christ, but their great contribution to American theology lay in pointing [newly converted Christians] to the prospect of a perfect adulthood in the Holy Spirit. From this point on in American Evangelicalism, the theology of Christian life became almost as important as the theology of Christian conversion.[17]

While the nature and extent of this Christian "perfection" would become a subject of much debate, Wesleyanism taught Christians that conversion did not mean the end of their dependence upon God.

After the end of the Second Awakening, revivals in America were smaller and more localized. The largest manifestations of the revivalistic spirit were associated with the ministry of evangelists like Charles G. Finney (1792–1875), Dwight L. Moody (1837–1899), Reuben A. Torrey (1856–1928), and Billy Sunday (1862–1935). Finney began the practice of large evangelistic rallies that would serve as forerunners of the crusades for which Billy Graham has become famous. Finney's ministry also provided a base for subsequent interest in a second Christian experience (usually called *sanctification*) following conversion that could help believers reach a condition of personal holiness. Dwight L. Moody did more than anyone else to shape the nature of evangelical revivalism during the second half of the nineteenth century. Converts at his huge rallies were invited to "come forward" at the end of the service and "make a decision for Christ." After 1925, revivalism in America went into a period of eclipse, until Billy Graham began to receive national attention around 1950.

Revivalism has been something of a mixed blessing for American Evangelicalism. It was instrumental in returning personal conversion and evangelism to evangelical faith and practice. It prodded Christians to take the deeper dimensions of Christian spirituality more seriously. But it was also the source of tensions that continue to divide evangelicals. As Evangelicalism moved into the twentieth century, movements such as Dispensationalism, Pentecostalism, and Fundamentalism, would provide grounds for additional divisions.

CHAPTER FOUR

The Breakdown of the Orthodox Consensus

The Catholic-Protestant consensus continued to be the dominant expression of Christian thought well into the nineteenth century. To whatever degree Catholics and Protestants disagreed over the issues raised by the Reformation, they continued to share a common world view that taught that this world was the creation of a personal, almighty God whose providence was manifest in history. They also agreed about the general historical reliability of the biblical picture of Jesus. They believed that Jesus was divine and that his miraculous birth was in fact the Incarnation, the event in which God entered the human race. They agreed about the general historical reliability of the teachings and miracles that the Gospels attributed to Jesus. They agreed that Jesus' death was a sacrifice for human sin that was followed by his miraculous resurrection from the dead.

But all this was to change in the second half of the nineteenth century. The Catholic-Protestant consensus came under attack not only from people outside the perimeter of the Christian church, but also from thinkers who continued to retain membership in various Christian denominations. To understand how this came to be, it is necessary to go back to the eighteenth century and examine the intellectual movement known as the Enlightenment.

The Enlightenment

The Enlightenment is the name given to a particular set of developments in philosophy, religion, and science that took place in eighteenth-century Europe. According to *The Oxford Dictionary of the Christian Church*, the Enlightenment combined

> opposition to all supernatural religion and belief in the all-sufficiency of human reason with an ardent desire to promote the happiness of men in this life. . . . Most of its representatives . . . rejected the Christian dogma and were hostile to Catholicism as well as Protestant orthodoxy, which they regarded as powers of spiritual darkness depriving humanity of the use of its rational faculties.[1]

This spirit of the Enlightenment made deep inroads into German Protestantism during the nineteenth century, where it helped to undermine confidence in the Scriptures. During the eighteenth century, the Enlightenment was characterized by skepticism in France, Rationalism in Germany, and Deism in England. The three controlling ideas of the Enlightenment were Reason, Nature, and Progress.

1. Reason

The Enlightenment was marked by an almost unbounded confidence in human reason. The natural sciences had just begun to push back the frontiers of human knowledge. People became excited at what they saw as the apparently unlimited powers of the human mind. But this growing confidence in human reason helped to produce a growing skepticism toward religious claims to truth. Those affected by the Enlightenment's rationalism became skeptical toward traditional religion, hostile toward faith, and uncertain in respect to authority. Human reason, the enlightened believed, could be trusted when the Bible and the church could not. The enlightened did not need the help of God or of the Bible or of the church in discovering truth. The ultimate authority for the enlightened became their own intellects. Even divine revelation must be subjected to the test of human reasoning. Deism, the most distinctive religious expression of the Enlightenment, denied God's active intervention in the world. This tended to rule out even the possibility of revelation, miracles, providence, and prayer. Deism sought a compromise between rationalism and Christianity by reducing religion to a few essentials that excluded the orthodox understanding of Jesus, of salvation, and of the Bible.

2. Nature

The second controlling principle of the Enlightenment was Nature. The preoccupation of the enlightened with this notion, coupled with their skepticism about traditional religion, led to Naturalism, the belief that the natural order is a completely closed system. In the world-view of the naturalist, the world is like a box with no openings. Everything that happens within the box must be caused by other events or conditions within the box. Not even God, if God should happen to exist, can break into the box and function as a cause within the natural order. On such a view, Christian supernaturalism must be false. The world is a tightly closed system that is not open to divine intervention. In contrast, Christian theism is supernatural, in the sense that it believes that the natural order is not ultimate, is not self-explanatory, and is not closed to the operations of God.

3. Progress

The Enlightenment was also characterized by a belief in progress. The enlightened believed that there was no limit to what the human race could accomplish. The Enlightenment produced an undisguised contempt for the human past and an unbounded optimism about the human future. In such a view in which human progress was inevitable, there was no room for the Christian understanding of human depravity. Therefore, a human race uncorrupted by sin had no need of a savior.

Some Consequences of the Enlightenment

While the Enlightenment did not at first destroy orthodoxy, it did remove orthodoxy from its central place as the unifier of Western life and culture. This happened in several different ways.

First, the Enlightenment created a climate within which unbelief could invade the church and begin the process that would lead to the collapse of the orthodox consensus. After the Enlightenment, doctrinal non-conformists and heretics, who formerly would have left the church or been expelled, began to teach their views within the church. To an increasing degree, unbelief began to set up residence within the church. "Despite the formal orthodoxy, or, better said, traditionalism, of most Protestant churches in the nineteenth century, dissenters found for the first time that they could disown basic Christian doctrines and still remain within the church, sometimes even retaining high church or academic posts."[2]

Second, during the nineteenth century, the after-effects of the Enlightenment helped lead to a repudiation or trivialization of the traditional role that truth had played in the Christian faith. The attack on the possibility of human knowledge about God had actually started in the work of David Hume (1711–1776) and Immanuel Kant (1724–1804), the most brilliant philosophers of the Enlightenment. As the effects of their philosophical arguments filtered down into the work of such Protestant theologians as Friedrich Schleiermacher (1768-1834) and Albrecht Ritschl (1822–1889), many

Christian thinkers began to deny that the major source of religious authority was an objectively true revelation from God in the Bible.[3] When theologians come to believe that knowledge about God is impossible and that religious truth is unimportant, it is only a matter of time until doctrines and creeds lose their relevance. Why worry about denials of Christian creeds if doctrine and truth are unimportant?

The authority of Scripture was undermined further by higher critical approaches to the Bible. One of the first targets of the higher critics was the Pentateuch, which was said to be a patchwork of several writers and editors that, in its final form, dates quite late in the history of Israel. Similar approaches to the Gospels served to undermine their value as historical documents.

Fallout from all this for the biblical picture of Jesus was not long in coming. While traditional Catholics and Protestants were aware of the difficulties of reconciling some parallel accounts in the Gospels, the problems were thought to be minor. There was little doubt but that the Gospels should be read as historical accounts of what Jesus did and said; there was general acceptance that these accounts were a faithful record of what had actually happened. But the growing spirit of unbelief and skepticism within Christendom produced distrust about the traditional Christian view of Jesus. Many liberals of the day assumed that the Gospels could no longer be read as reliable historical documents whose picture of Jesus could be accepted at face value. For such thinkers, the Gospels contained errors, myths, and even outright lies that needed to be stripped away by the methods of literary and historical criticism. Consequently, a number of liberal nineteenth-century scholars began to produce liberal biographies of Jesus that picked their way through the source materials so as to leave a picture of Jesus that would be compatible with the scholar's humanistic and naturalistic presuppositions.[4]

Even though Charles Darwin's theory of evolution belonged

to the nineteenth century, it fit naturally into the mind-set that developed after the Enlightenment. Darwin provided intellectuals with a theory about the origin and development of the human race that matched such Enlightenment presuppositions as the belief in inevitable human progress. What began as a scientific hypothesis about the origin of the species turned into a religious dogma that human biological ascendance would be paralleled by equally spectacular improvements in moral and religious life.

A Fatal Weakness in Nineteenth-Century Evangelicalism

The drift toward religious skepticism and unbelief within the nineteenth-century church was helped by the intellectual developments that have already been noted. But it was also aided by a condition that had developed within Evangelicalism. The religious revivals of the nineteenth century had little impact on the intellectual life of the church. Because they left the mind of the revived church largely untouched, the revivals or awakenings did not produce any resurgence of theological orthodoxy. In earlier centuries, orthodoxy had benefitted from its links with the university world. But during the nineteenth century, orthodoxy became increasingly isolated from centers of intellectual activity. A strong commitment to the authority of the Bible, along with a continuing belief in supernaturalism, characterized most of American Christianity through the first half of the nineteenth century. But American Christians were becoming increasingly derelict in their responsibility to provide an intellectual defense of their faith. The revivals of the nineteenth century "rejected the naturalistic religion of Deism as well as the skepticism of the Enlightenment, but did not refute them. The challenge that man's mind had raised was answered by an appeal to his heart. The modern mentality that had undermined faith was countered with an equally modern sentimentality, rather than with a renewal of the Christian mentality."[5]

The pietism that the nineteenth-century revivals tended to produce triumphed over skepticism with religious enthusiasm but failed totally to counter that skepticism with arguments. As the nineteenth century drew to a close, Evangelicalism's inattention to the life of the mind helped leave it defenseless against its enemies. The collapse of the orthodox consensus was just a matter of time.

CHAPTER FIVE

Fundamentalism

The stage is now set for a discussion of Fundamentalism. Since Fundamentalism began as a reaction to the liberal tendencies that began to appear in the second half of the nineteenth century, it is important to review the significant ways in which liberalism changed the nature of the Christian faith. As rationalism, skepticism, and anti-supernaturalism became widespread in Christendom, a number of Christian thinkers began to modify Christian thinking along the lines of their reinterpretation of Christianity.

The new theological ideas that came to be called religious modernism or Protestant liberalism spread rapidly throughout Europe and gradually began to influence religious thinking in America. The impact of this German liberalism on American theology was made even greater because of other things going on in the intellectual life of America, tendencies already mentioned in chapter four. The early Christian consensus was now being challenged inside the walls of institutional Christendom.

Emilio Núñez provides an excellent short summary of the new liberal theology:

> Liberalism not only tried to undermine faith in the cardinal doctrines of the church; it was also intensely humanistic in the sense that it believed man to be essentially good and fully able to solve his problems and build for himself a better world. The

liberals were characterized by their great faith in human progress. They seemed to be incurably optimistic. Their theology gave the impression that God was present in the wonderful world of science and technology, working for the benefit of man. They emphasized the immanence of God, passing over His transcendence. They placed the religion of feeling above the authority of written revelation. They subjected the Bible to the judgment of reason in the way they applied historical and literary criticism to it, denying the possibility that God could reveal Himself in a supernatural way through the Scriptures. Thus the liberals sacrificed the Bible's authority on the altar of human reason.[1]

The liberal deviation from the classical Christian view of God and man was coupled with an equally serious distortion of the orthodox view of Jesus Christ. As James Packer explains, for liberalism: "Jesus Christ is man's Savior only in the sense that He is man's perfect Teacher and Example. We should regard Him simply as the first Christian, our elder brother in the world-wide family of God. He was not divine in any unique sense. He was God only in the sense that He was a perfectly God-conscious and God-guided man. He was not born of a virgin; He did not work miracles, in the sense of mighty works of divine creative power; and He did not rise from the dead."[2]

The liberal's substitution of these new beliefs for the traditional Christian understanding of God, Jesus, humanity, and the Bible led naturally to a new view for Christianity's place among the religions of the world.

> Just as Christ differs from other men only comparatively, not absolutely, so Christianity differs from other religions not generally, but merely as the best and highest type of religion that has yet appeared. All religions are forms of the same religion, just as all men are members of the same divine family. It follows, of course, that Foreign Missions should not aim to convert from one faith to another, but rather to promote a

cross-fertilizing interchange whereby each religion may be enriched through the contribution of all others.[3]

Liberalism was a religion without a personal God, without a divine Savior, without an inspired Bible, and without a transforming conversion. This new religion, however, proceeded to capture control of denominational schools, publications, missions, boards, and eventually total control of the mainline denominations. In mainline colleges and seminaries, professors of religion denied practically every tenet of the orthodox consensus. The new religion had captured control of the institutional church.

The Rise and Decline of Fundamentalism

Generally speaking, conservative Protestants in the nineteenth century were rather slow to respond to the growing liberal movement. To some extent, this was due to the fact that liberalism at first developed slowly and quietly. And, as pointed out in the last chapter, Evangelicalism had failed to give much importance to the life of the mind. Things began to change when conservatives began to realize that many of their schools, institutions, and churches were being lost to the rationalized brand of Christianity.

What became known as Fundamentalism began as part of the general evangelical reaction to the liberalism that threatened the integrity of the historic Christian faith. Conservatives agreed that whatever liberalism was, it certainly was not Christianity. It was a betrayal of everything that historic Christianity had stood for. Liberalism was a totally new religion that its proponents were trying to pass off on an unsuspecting church through the use of traditional language and labels.

In its early years, Fundamentalism showed some promise. Theological discussions by early fundamentalists were conducted at a generally high level. Between 1890 and about 1920, a number of competent conservative scholars wrote books and articles that challenged the inroads that liberalism was making in the mainline churches. These conservative scholars included James Orr, a respected Scottish theologian, and several professors at Princeton Theological Seminary, such as Benjamin Warfield, R. Dick Wilson, and J. Gresham Machen.

During the earliest years of the conservative debate with liberalism, no one was called a fundamentalist. The term did not enter the language as a name for the movement until after 1910. To some extent, the growing use of the label was connected with the publication of a series of twelve small volumes called *The Fundamentals*. Financed through the gifts of two wealthy laymen, this publishing project continued from 1910 to 1915. By the early 1920s, many conservative Protestants were proudly calling themselves fundamentalists. They were convinced that without the fundamental doctrines that liberalism had rejected, historic Christianity could not survive.

During the 1920s, liberals were increasingly successful in excluding conservatives from positions of power. In denomination after denomination, the power structure came under the control of people whose theology was inconsistent with that of historic Christianity. To some extent, the consolidation of liberal control was aided by clergy and laypeople who, though theologically conservative, appeared to compromise important convictions as they placed their denomination or personal interests ahead of God's truth. At least, this is how some conservatives interpreted their reluctance to enter the battle.

In the minds of many Americans, the famous Scopes trial that took place in Cleveland, Tennessee, in 1925 became the symbol of Fundamentalism's final defeat. While the legal battle was won by William Jennings Bryan and the anti-evolution forces, the real winner, in the minds of those who followed the case, was the evolutionist cause, led by Clarence

Darrow. The media painted the fundamentalists as militant anti-intellectuals out of step with modern science and culture. Liberalism had now begun to win the important public relations battle.

In the decades that followed, many conservatives came to view the Scopes trial and its aftermath with misgivings. There were much better ways, many of them thought, to combat whatever genuine threat to orthodoxy might be contained in various theories of evolution. These later conservatives recognized the danger in allowing one particular interpretation of a biblical passage to settle in the public's mind the question of the truth of the entire Bible. William Jennings Bryan did not begin to have the biblical, scientific, and philosophical training to become orthodoxy's spokesman in a public debate over such a complex and emotional issue.

By the end of the 1930s, mainline liberals were congratulating themselves that Fundamentalism was dying and that all that remained was to set the date for the funeral. But the fundamentalists had a surprise up their sleeve. Like the phoenix of Egyptian mythology, Fundamentalism would rise renewed from its ashes. But this rebirth of Fundamentalism would take several decades and would, in the process, alter the nature of Fundamentalism and give rise to the Evangelicalism that is the subject of this book.

Divisions Within Fundamentalism

When it began, Fundamentalism was a necessary reaction to the unbelief that had settled in the mainline denominations. As Fundamentalism developed, however, serious weaknesses soon became apparent, hindering the effectiveness of its defense and proclamation of the gospel. It began to evidence a number of characteristics that would eventually lead many to leave the fold. James Packer describes what happened:

Fundamentalism withdrew more and more into the shell provided by its own interdenominational organizations. Partly in self-defence, the movement developed a pronounced anti-intellectual bias; it grew distrustful of scholarship, sceptical as to the value of reasoning in matters of religion and truculent in its attitude towards the arguments of its opponents. Something less than intellectual integrity appeared in its readiness to support a good cause with a bad argument. Its apologetics were makeshift, piecemeal and often unprincipled and unsound. Its adventures in the field of the natural sciences, especially with reference to evolution, were most unfortunate. Here, where the Fundamentalists' confidence was greatest, their competence was least, and their performance brought ridicule and discredit on themselves. Generally, Fundamentalism lacked theological energy and concern for Christian learning. It grew intellectually barren. Culture became suspect. The responsibilities of Christian social witness were left to the purveyors of the "social gospel", and Fundamentalism turned in upon itself, limiting its interests to evangelism and the cultivation of personal religion.[4]

As Fundamentalism became increasingly associated with ignorance, rudeness, combativeness, anti-intellectualism, and cultural isolationism, many conservative Protestants understandably became uneasy about being identified with such traits. They also became uncomfortable with the growing fundamentalist tendency to make certain minor or non-essential beliefs and practices into tests of orthodoxy and Christian fellowship.

The unfortunate excess to which Fundamentalism became prone produced two waves of dissent within the fundamentalist camp. During the first wave, which began shortly after the end of World War II, a number of former fundamentalists grew disenchanted with the movement within which their personal faith had begun and been nourished. To distinguish themselves from Fundamentalism, these conservative Christians returned to the older label of Evangelicalism.[5]

The second wave of fundamentalist dissent was led by Jerry Falwell and his followers, beginning in the late 1970s. While the first wave led to a distinction between fundamentalists and evangelicals, the second wave produced a division between what can be called the New Fundamentalism of Jerry Falwell and the Old Fundamentalism that is still represented by Bob Jones University.

Many people would find it difficult to imagine circumstances under which anyone could regard Billy Graham as a liberal. But fundamentalist denunciations of Graham came to symbolize the first wave that led to the break between Fundamentalism and Evangelicalism. The even more incredible allegation that Jerry Falwell is liberal serves to capture the essence of the growing split between the new and old forms of Fundamentalism. The charge that Jerry Falwell is "the most dangerous man in America" came, not from the head of the American Civil Liberties Union, but from the president of Bob Jones University, the prototype of old-style, hard-line Fundamentalism.

The First Wave of Dissent: Evangelicalism

The Protestant conservatives who decided to break with Fundamentalism after World War II were, to a large degree, attempting to rid themselves of a label that had become weighted down by too many negative connotations. They also recognized that *Fundamentalism* was a twentieth-century name for a set of beliefs that had roots going back to the early Christian consensus and the writings of the New Testament. Because of their conscious attempt to return to the classical Evangelicalism of earlier centuries, it was natural for these conservatives to regard *evangelical* as a much more appropriate label for their position.

During much of the 1950s and 1960s, Fundamentalism and Evangelicalism often appeared to be two entirely separate movements. Insiders, of course, knew how much they continued to have in common theologically. But many of the harshest criticisms of each movement came from the other. One prominent evangelical author who decided to worship in a fundamentalist church while on a trip found himself in a Sunday school class that was studying the great heresies of the twentieth century. Ironically, he discovered, the subject on that particular Sunday was himself. Deriving what profit he could from the denunciations of his views, he kept his identity a secret.

For almost thirty years, then, Fundamentalism and Evangelicalism have been distinct, though overlapping, religious movements. Anyone clearly identified as an evangelical was unwelcome in the camp of the true fundamentalists. Fundamentalists and evangelicals had their own schools, publications, and in many cases, their own denominations. In a few instances, such as the Conservative Baptist Association, fundamentalists and evangelicals carried on a running battle with each other. One of the few points of contact was the Evangelical Theological Society (founded in 1949).

As noted earlier, evangelicals objected to many features of modern Fundamentalism, including its anti-intellectualism and belligerency. Many old-line fundamentalists often elevated a number of minor doctrines to a point where they became tests of orthodoxy and fellowship. In such a view, for example, it was not enough to believe in the Second Coming of Christ. It was also necessary to subscribe to a specific interpretation of Christ's return along with a detailed chronology of the precise order in which prophetic events would occur.

The importance that fundamentalists placed upon their interpretation of biblical passages dealing with the Second Coming had a great deal to do with their acceptance of a position known as *Dispensationalism.* While not everyone who might be called a fundamentalist is necessarily a dispensationalist, it is possible to see how the two movements have joined hands throughout the twentieth century. The doctrinal statements of many fundamentalist schools still require an acceptance of basic dispensationalist tenets.

Basic to the dispensational approach to the Bible are the sharp distinctions it draws between the different ways God has dealt with human beings during different periods of time. While dispensationalists usually distinguish seven such dispensations, the two most important are the Dispensation of Law (from the giving of the Mosaic Law to the beginning of the Christian Church at Pentecost) and the Dispensation of Grace (the entire church age that will end with the Rapture of the Church). In connection with the periods of Law and Grace, it is also important to distinguish between the quite different ways in which God dealt with the most important groups of people in those two dispensations: the nation of Israel (Law) and the Church (Grace). One of the quickest ways to misinterpret the Bible, dispensationalists argue, is to take a verse that was meant for one group (such as Israel) and apply it to the other (such as the Church). Dispensational extremists often seemed to work on the boundaries of heresy as when, for example, some of them suggested that in some dispensations human salvation depended on good works. Non-dispensationalists objected to a method of biblical interpretation that divided the household of God into different segments, each of which could be saved in a different way. For the non-dispensationalist, Abraham, Moses, and David were saved in precisely the same way every Christian is saved, namely by faith (Romans 4:1-25). In fairness, less extreme dispensationalists shied away from suggestions that God saved people in different ways in different dispensations.

Most fundamentalists took a position regarding the Second Coming known as Pre-millennialism. The word *millennium* refers to the period of one thousand years mentioned in Revelation 20:1-10. A pre-millennialist interprets that passage literally and, therefore, believes that Christ will actually rule this planet for a thousand years some time in the future. What makes this person a *pre*-millennialist is the additional belief that Christ's Second Coming will occur before the establishing of the earthly millennial kingdom.

But no true dispensationalist can be satisfied with the bare acceptance of pre-millennialism. Dispensational fundamentalists must also be pre-tribulationists. In their blueprint of the end times, the next event in the prophetic calendar is the Rapture. While this event resembles the Second Coming, it must never be confused with it. In the Rapture, Christ will return in the clouds for the entire Christian church. Dead believers will be restored to life and caught up in the air, where they will join with living believers who have been transformed. None of this will be visible to the unbelieving world that will be left behind following the Rapture. All that unbelievers will know is that suddenly every Christian in the world has disappeared. The Rapture will not only mark the end of the Dispensation of Grace (the church age), but it will also usher in the most terrible period of time the world has ever known, the Great Tribulation. A great evil world leader, the Anti-Christ, will gain control of the world. People who become believers during the Tribulation will suffer terrible persecution; many thousands of them will be martyred. The world will experience numerous natural catastrophes (famines, plagues, and earthquakes) along with the war that will finally end all wars. Finally, at the end of the seven-year Tribulation period, the armies of the world will gather at a place called Armaggedon. At this time, Christ will return (this is the *real* Second Coming) with the armies of heaven, destroy the wicked, and set up his millennial kingdom.

While evangelicals believe in a literal Second Coming, most find it regrettable that many people think the dispensationalist, pre-tribulational theory just outlined is the only view permitted by careful biblical exegesis. One reason for the widespread acceptance of the view is its prominence in the footnotes of the *Scofield Reference Bible*. The theory reached millions of other people through the best-selling book *The Late Great Planet Earth* by Hal Lindsey.

A number of other options are available. For example, some people remain pre-millennialists but adopt a post-tribulation position in the sense that they believe Christ will return for his church at the end of the Tribulation period. A few evangelicals have returned to a popular nineteenth century view known as *Post-millennialism*. They believe that Christ's Second Coming will occur *after* the thousand year period described in Revelation 20. Some of those evangelicals known as Reconstructionists believe it is the church's duty not to abandon the present age to apostasy and godlessness but to work to reestablish kingdom principles and laws on earth.[6] Whether post-millennialists belong to the Reconstructionist movement, all of them believe they have a God-given obligation to try to change the world for the better.

A growing number of former pre-millennialists are attracted by the position known as Amillennialism, which interprets the thousand years of Revelation 20 in a nonliteral way. For an amillennialist, there will be no literal thousand year reign of Christ on earth. When this age ends, there will be only one return of Christ to earth, to be followed immediately by the Great White Throne Judgment where God will finally and forever separate believers from unbelievers.[7]

The point to this lengthy detour into Bible prophecy is that one of the major differences between Fundamentalism and Evangelicalism is the fundamentalist's continuing insistence that only one interpretation is permissible; the plea of most evangelicals is for greater tolerance in this difficult area.

Protestant conservatism in America split into two distinct camps during the 1950s. The evangelicals no longer wanted to be thought of as fundamentalists. And many fundamentalists denounced the evangelicals as traitors to the Christian cause. Evangelicals like Billy Graham became targets of fundamentalist attacks. But during the years in which many fundamentalists and evangelicals stopped talking to one another, Fundamentalism was changing in other ways that would eventually produce the second wave of dissent.

The Second Wave of Dissent: The New Fundamentalism

The major issue that led to the rupture between New and Old Fundamentalism was separatism. Separatism had been a dominant feature of Fundamentalism since at least the 1930s. The central idea of separatism can be found in a favorite fundamentalist text, II Corinthians 6:17: "Therefore come out from them and be separate, says the Lord. Touch no unclean thing, and I will receive you." Of course, in its New Testament context, the verse was a warning to Christians who lived in a godless, immoral city not to become involved in the wickedness of their neighbors. Taken in that sense, of course, the verse has continuing relevance for Christians of all ages. But when pulled out of context, the verse gave impetus to the fundamentalist practice of separatism. Christians were also to separate themselves from anyone who was not properly fundamentalist in their belief or conduct. At first, this meant that Christians (fundamentalists) should separate themselves from liberals. Then it was used to mean that fundamentalists should separate themselves from evangelicals like Billy Graham who had refused to separate themselves from liberals. Finally, the text was used to urge true fundamentalists to separate themselves from "compromising" fundamentalists, like Jerry Falwell.

Because this subject is so complicated and so important, with regard to understanding the most recent division within Fundamentalism, it deserves further analysis. Separatism evolved into a doctrine where several orders of separation were at stake. In the case of first-order separatism, every fundamentalist is obliged to remain separate from unbelievers and from ungodly or worldly people. In second-order separatism, true fundamentalists are urged to remain separate from those believers who fellowship with people who fellowship with unbelievers or the ungodly. In third-order separatism, faithful fundamentalists were supposed also to remain separate from believers who failed to practice second-order separatism.

By the time the separatist extremists reached the third stage of separation, Jerry Falwell and other fundamentalists decided it was time to object, especially since they were the ones denounced for failing to practice third-order separatism. Falwell, by the late 1970s, felt called to reintroduce the fundamentalist message and values back into the mainstream of American life. Falwell was proud of his fundamentalist heritage and the fundamentalist label. But Falwell found himself somewhere in the middle between the evangelicals, whom he suspected of some liberalism and compromise, and the old, hard-line fundamentalists who would have nothing to do with anyone who cooperated with Roman Catholics and Jews, even in the cause of restoring moral values to the country. By the early 1980s, the die was cast and it was too late to turn back. In the early issues of *The Fundamentalist Journal* and in his book *The Fundamentalist Phenomenon*, Falwell and his associates announced to the world that a New Fundamentalism had been born. Actually, they argued, their Fundamentalism was not new; they were going to revive the Fundamentalism of the past. All of this proved to be quite interesting to students of Evangelicalism, the first wave of dissent. With few exceptions, most notably Falwell's retention of the fundamentalist label, many of his announced goals were similar to those of evangelical leaders in the years between 1945 and 1955. What was also interesting to note was that

Evangelicalism, itself, had been going through inner turmoil. As subsequent discussions will indicate, Evangelicalism had been dividing into a liberal and a more conservative wing. As things stand now in the mid-1980s, it is increasingly difficult to see any significant differences between the conservative wing of the evangelical movement and Falwell's "liberal" wing of the fundamentalist movement.

The relations between the New Fundamentalism and the broader evangelical movement have become rather complex. To a large extent, this complexity reflects the growing diversity of mainstream Evangelicalism. Because of an increasing recognition of common interests, more conservative evangelicals and Falwell's branch of the fundamentalist movement are exploring ways of achieving greater unity. Some of the new fundamentalists are even admitting that Fundamentalism has occasionally erred. Ed Dobson, editor of *The Fundamentalist Journal* has acknowledged: "Too often fundamentalists have been characterized by negativism, pessimism, extreme separatism, and exclusivism. We have been known more for what we are *against* than what we are *for.*"[9]

But the new fundamentalists continue to have their problems with evangelicals, at least with some evangelicals. They chide evangelicals for being more preoccupied with gaining respectability than with winning souls. While evangelicals have made remarkable strides, gaining acceptance for their movement, their institutions, and themselves, fundamentalists have continued to "win souls" and build huge churches. While faithfulness to God should never be equated with numbers, the fundamentalists may have a point in their claim that many evangelicals have lost a zeal for evangelism. The new fundamentalists also criticize evangelicals for a growing laxness on a few theological beliefs, most notably the doctrine of Scripture.

Some evangelicals believe a major realignment is taking

place within Evangelicalism. They see a growing split between the more liberal and conservative factions of mainstream Evangelicalism and a developing rapprochement between new fundamentalists and conservative mainstream evangelicals. If this continues, old-line fundamentalists will become even more isolated than in the past. What will happen to evangelicals who are more liberal theologically is more difficult to say.

CHAPTER SIX

Pentecostalism

The third major subculture of contemporary Evangelicalism is the charismatic movement or Pentecostalism. The words *charismatic* and *pentecostal* scare the daylights out of many mainline and evangelical Christians. To the uninformed, the words produce images of uncontrolled people rolling down church aisles or swinging from the chandeliers or lapsing into comas after shouting something in an unknown language. But even people who have learned to ignore such stereotypes still worry about the often schismatic element of Pentecostalism; many churches have been badly divided over what is supposed to have been a movement of God's Spirit.

Basic to movements and people who can be called charismatic or pentecostal is an experience or set of experiences that such people associate with the work of the Holy Spirit. One Roman Catholic pentecostal defines charismatics as "born-again Christians who accept the Bible as an inspired Word of God and who believe they are emphasizing a part of Christian tenet that is often neglected by other Bible believers, namely, the power of the Holy Spirit, the Baptism of the Holy Spirit, and the Gifts of the Holy Spirit."[1]

Pentecostalism is no longer limited to a small segment of North American Protestants. The number of pentecostals in the world is now estimated to be fifty million, spread among eighty nations.[2] In Latin America, pentecostals make up the majority of Protestants. There is also a growing charismatic movement among American Roman Catholics that, according to some estimates, now numbers six million.

The word *charismatic* comes from the Greek word *charisma*, used in the New Testament to denote the spiritual gifts God gave the early church. The basic New Testament passage that discusses these gifts is the twelfth chapter of I Corinthians. Paul begins by mentioning that there are many different kinds of gifts, but that all are made possible by the same Spirit of God (verse 4).

> To one there is given through the Spirit the message of wisdom, to another the message of knowledge by means of the same Spirit, to another faith by the same Spirit, to another gifts of healing by that one Spirit, to another miraculous powers, to another prophecy, to another the ability to distinguish between spirits, to another the ability to speak in different kinds of tongues, and to still another the interpretation of tongues. (I Corinthians 12:8-10)

The Christian church has disagreed sharply over the meaning and continuing relevance of first-century gifts. Some think the gifts were a first-century phenomenon, given largely to help the young church get started. A charismatic is someone who believes the special gifts are still available to the contemporary church and should be utilized by Spirit-filled Christians.

The word *pentecostal* is derived from the Day of Pentecost, when the descent of the Holy Spirit upon the tiny group of Christian believers was accompanied by many marvelous signs. Christians spoke in other languages; the sick were healed; and other miracles were performed. In its twentieth-century usage, *pentecostal* refers to manifestations of the power and signs associated with the original Pentecost in the lives of contemporary believers.

77

Two phrases that usually occur in any discussion of the charismatic movement are "the baptism of the Holy Spirit" and "speaking in tongues" (*glossolalia*). The baptism of the Holy Spirit is explained as "a second encounter with God (the first being conversion) in which the Christian begins to receive the power of the Holy Spirit into his/her life; for most Pentecostals and many neo-Pentecostals, the evidence of having been baptized by the Holy Spirit is glossolalia."[3]

Non-charismatics differ sharply with such claims. They argue that the New Testament uses the word *baptism* in two basically different ways: (1) to refer to water baptism (Acts 1:5) and (2) to refer to the divine act by which every believer is joined to Christ. The phrase, "the baptism of the Spirit," these non-charismatics insist, applies properly only to something that takes place at conversion (I Corinthians 12:13; Ephesians 4:5). Charismatics remain unconvinced by such arguments. After all, they and other pentecostals have had a transforming post-conversion experience. It is natural, they think, to associate their experience with John the Baptist's promise that while he baptized only with water, the one who followed him (Jesus) would baptize "with the Holy Spirit and with fire" (Matthew 3:11). Non-charismatics reply that texts like Matthew 3:11 only appear to support the pentecostal cause and that charismatics are guilty of reading conclusions drawn from their experiences into such verses. It seems safe to predict that a resolution of this disagreement will not occur in the near future.

The most distinctive characteristic of the charismatic movement is speaking in tongues. As one pentecostal explains, the baptism of the Spirit "means the experience of being filled by the Lord with the Spirit to the point that the Spirit can articulate through him in another language—unlearned—the praise and glory of God."[4] For pentecostals, the gift of tongues means the ability to pray or speak in a non-earthly or heavenly language, the meaning of which is unknown to them or anyone else. In such a view, speaking in tongues is "a form of nondiscursive prayer in an unintelligible language."[5] Non-charismatics object to the importance that pentecostals place upon tongues. They point out that Paul subordinated speaking in tongues to the more important gift of speaking the gospel (prophecy): "He who prophesies is greater than one who speaks in tongues, unless he interprets, so that the church may be edified" (I Corinthians 14:5). Paul also declared that love is far superior to speaking in tongues: "If I speak in the tongues of men and of angels, but have not love, I am only a resounding gong or a clanging cymbal" (I Corinthians 13:1). Paul also advised the church about the importance of such languages being interpreted, which seems to belie the pentecostal claim that proper tongues speaking occurs in unknown languages (I Corinthians 14:5). Pentecostals themselves disagree about the necessity of the tongues experience. While most of them regard speaking in tongues as the one certain sign of Spirit baptism, a minority of pentecostals view tongues as an important, but unnecessary, piece of evidence that someone has received the baptism. Some non-pentecostals argue that the gift of tongues in the early church was simply the divinely given ability of some Christians to preach the gospel in a language previously unknown to him. Naturally, twentieth-century Christians who have actually had the tongues experience reject that interpretation.

It is helpful to distinguish between an Old and New Pentecostalism. The Old Pentecostalism is often said to have begun around 1900 in Topeka, Kansas, when a number of students at Bethel Bible College began to speak in tongues. Although rejected by mainline churches, the tongues movement spread to Texas and to such large cities as Los Angeles, Chicago, and New York. The Old Pentecostalism was color-blind, as whites within the movement fellowshiped and shared their experience with a growing number of black pentecostals.

Old Pentecostalism suffered from a number of problems. Sociologically, it was a movement that had its greatest influence among lower class and poorly educated people. Perhaps, for this reason, it often was characterized by behavioral excesses. During pentecostal services, people often appeared to become possessed and lose control physically and emotionally. Many old pentecostals evidenced a disturbing lack of interest in doctrinal matters. Repeating "the experience" was usually far more important than serious Bible study or reflection on the doctrinal content of the Christian faith. This led to instances in which the pentecostal experience was shared by people who advocated such heresies as unitarianism.

Some of the "gifts" were faked by charlatans who preyed on the gullibility of those who thought that any manifestation of the charismatic gifts automatically certified the preacher or "healer" as a man or woman of God. But alongside these unfortunate characteristics, there was also a growing base of solid evangelical believers who began to combine their emphasis upon the pentecostal experience with serious Bible study and church membership. Significant growth began to take place within the Assemblies of God, the first pentecostal denomination (organized in 1914), and some of the other thirty-five pentecostal denominations in the United States.

The recent developments that have produced the New Pentecostalism (or Neo-pentecostalism) are significant because of the changes they are making in the way charismatics practice their faith and in the way they are viewed by non-charismatics. For one thing, the new pentecostals are much more circumspect in their behavior; they tend to avoid many of the excesses of earlier pentecostals. Moreover, the New Pentecostalism is a movement among middle and upper-class people who are much better educated than earlier groups of pentecostals. And finally, Neo-pentecostalism is a movement taking place largely within mainline and evangelical churches that were previously off-limits to the pentecostal experience. The New Pentecostalism is bringing the charismatic movement into the mainstream of American Christianity.

New Pentecostalism is often said to have started in St. Mark's Episcopal Church in Van Nuys, California, in 1960. The rector of St. Mark's, Dennis Bennett, received the baptism of the Spirit and the gift of tongues. Sharing his experience with his congregation, Bennett soon found that many members of his church were being converted and also receiving the baptism, including the gift of tongues. This did not sit well with Bennett's superiors, who moved him to a small mission church in Seattle, not expecting that similar occurrences would soon produce a spiritual awakening in the new church. Bennett's new church grew phenomenally as he and his new congregation spread their neo-pentecostal message in the northwest.

Neo-pentecostalism reached the Roman Catholic church during a February, 1967, meeting at Duquesne University in Pittsburgh. It spread rapidly, first to the campus of the University of Notre Dame and then to Ann Arbor, Michigan. Today, it is said, there are approximately six million charismatic Roman Catholics in the United States.[6]

An important means of spreading the charismatic message is the Full Gospel Businessmen's Fellowship. Started in the 1950s, it now has over two thousand local chapters in more than seventy nations. While helping to strengthen representatives of the older pentecostal movement, the Fellowship has been instrumental in spreading the "full gospel" of Pentecostalism to mainline churches. The charismatic message is also actively promoted over the PTL and CBN cable television networks. Both Jim Bakker (PTL) and Pat Robertson (CBN) are neo-pentecostals.

Non-charismatics point out that, like any religious movement, Pentecostalism needs to be careful about a number of potential trouble spots. One of these concerns the ever-present danger of overemphasizing the emotional side of religion to the exclusion of objective checks and reference points. One classic (old) pentecostal, William G. MacDonald, has commented on this. In his view, Pentecostalism should not worry about emotionalism in the sense of feeling strong religious emotions. Any religion, he points out, that did not touch people's emotions would be incomplete in important respects. But there is another sense of emotionalism about which pentecostals should be concerned. This is the kind of emotionalism that

> consists of the seeking and stimulation of emotions as ends in themselves, and not as the by-products of real experience in truth and in God. Emotionalism in this pejorative sense is of the flesh, and we do not claim that there have not been those among us who were culpable of mistaking effects for causes in this manner. However, we would assert unequivocally that any genuine experience with the living God will leave an emotional wake in a man's psyche. This is not emotionalism but man's being humanized again by the liberating Spirit of God.[7]

Charismatics also need to beware of the danger of elevating personal experience above the normative and objective revelation God has given in Scripture. Human experience, like church tradition, must constantly be tested by the objective truth found in God's Word.

Non-charismatics also object to what they see as an unscriptural emphasis that pentecostals place on speaking in tongues. When pentecostals declare that tongues are a necessary sign of Spirit baptism, they unthinkingly imply that Christian leaders—such as Martin Luther, John Calvin, John Wesley, George Whitefeld, D. L. Moody, and Billy Graham—accomplished all that they did for God without the baptism of the Holy Spirit. The world is still waiting for a pentecostal who will match their achievements.

Pentecostals also need to give more attention to the life of the mind, including the study of systematic theology. The small unitarian movement among people who manifest all of the usual charismatic gifts is a problem that pentecostals cannot ignore. Charismatics can hardly claim that the possession of charismatic gifts is an automatic certification of conversion and Spirit baptism, when those gifts are practiced by unitarians whose denial of the deity of Christ means they fail an important biblical test that must be met before anyone should be considered a Christian. It seems clear that a person can manifest the charismatic gifts without necessarily being baptized with the Spirit or being a Christian in the New Testament sense. At the same time, many non-charismatics are thankful for any genuine movement of God's Spirit in the church that will give lethargic Christians new life and power.

CHAPTER SEVEN

Some Representative Evangelicals

Evangelicalism is represented by so many different individuals, each representing his or her own constituency, that one often needs a scorecard to tell who is playing for which team. The purpose of this chapter is to select a small number of evangelicals who can serve as representatives of the movement as a whole and provide some information about their background. The selection is made from the perspective of the mid-1980s. Twenty years ago, such a list would have been quite different. The basis of the selection is simple: which evangelicals, living or dead, continue to have the greatest influence on Evangelicalism as it approaches the twenty-first century?

Billy Graham

No one can dispute Billy Graham's inclusion in this list. The non-evangelical world views Graham as Evangelicalism's chief ambassador. Informed evangelicals, of course, understand that this is an oversimplification, in the sense that no one person could possibly speak for a movement as individualistic and diverse as Evangelicalism. But Graham comes as close to doing this as anyone.

William Franklin Graham, Jr. was born in Charlotte, North Carolina, in 1918. Converted in his late teens, Graham attended two fundamentalist schools, including Bob Jones University, before making his way to Wheaton College, just west of Chicago. After graduating from Wheaton in 1943, he served briefly as pastor of a small church in a Chicago suburb before becoming an evangelist with the newly formed Youth for Christ organization. In the late 1940s, Graham and an evangelistic team that included songleader Cliff Barrows and singer George Beverly Shea began to conduct revivals around the country. Nothing particularly noteworthy happened to this evangelistic ministry until Graham's now famous Los Angeles revival in 1949. Although the crusade was originally scheduled to last three weeks, the large crowds and many conversions resulted in the meeting's being extended to eight weeks. During that time, approximately three hundred fifty thousand people heard Graham preach, and about three thousand were converted, including a number of well-known personalities from the entertainment industry. Graham and his crusade became front-page news.

The Los Angeles crusade was followed almost immediately by another in Boston, Massachusetts. The response to the Boston meetings was so overwhelming that the crusade had to be moved from historic Park Street Church on the Boston Common to a six thousand-seat auditorium. At the final service in the sixteen thousand-seat Boston Garden, about ten thousand people had to be turned away. Within a few months, Graham was preaching regularly to audiences numbering forty thousand and more. When his crusades in England and in such non-Christian nations as India attracted even larger audiences, it was clear that something important was going on. In 1957, Graham's team took on the challenge of ministering to New York City. Many skeptics believed that Graham's message and style would meet their match in Godless New York. But they were wrong.

Graham's well-organized crusades became the foundation of

a ministry that includes a nation-wide radio broadcast ("The Hour of Decision") and a film company that makes and distributes movies with a distinctively evangelical message. For more than a decade, Graham's organization has produced hour-long television programs, taped from his more important city-wide crusades, that are broadcast nationally. By the early 1980s, Graham's ministry had covered the globe, including services in the Soviet Union and other Eastern bloc nations.

Graham is no more infallible than any other human being. Because of his constant media attention, his occasional gaffes have been moderately embarrassing. Graham admits somewhat ruefully that in the past he may have been too closely associated with some American presidents and other people in high places. But no one doubts Graham's integrity and his commitment to the gospel. Graham has repeatedly refused to abandon evangelism for a career in public life. Because he has always drawn a salary from the Billy Graham Organization, there has never been any question about his profiting personally from the huge amounts of money required to fund his crusades.

Hard-line fundamentalists have been Graham's harshest critics. While assorted liberals have made fun of Graham's conservative theology for several years, many have come to respect him personally and even to appreciate the renewal that his crusades have brought to the church. But for old-time fundamentalists, Graham came to symbolize compromise and ultimate betrayal of the gospel. The problem, of course, is Graham's practice of allowing his crusades to be supported by liberal Protestants and even Roman Catholics. Graham's thought is that he will preach the gospel to anyone who will listen and sees nothing wrong when a Roman Catholic archbishop commends his crusade.

Whatever future historians of the Christian church may say about some of the other representative evangelicals in this chapter, Graham's influence on Evangelicalism and on twentieth-century Christianity has been enormous.

Jerry Falwell

If Billy Graham is Mr. Evangelicalism, then Jerry Falwell is Mr. Fundamentalism. Of course, Falwell's name often generates a different and much more negative response than does Graham's. To some extent, this fact reflects important differences between Evangelicalism and Fundamentalism. But it also evidences some unfortunate misunderstandings of the man and how he has grown.

Falwell was born in 1933 in Lynchburg, Virginia. After a conversion experience in his teens, Falwell attended Baptist Bible College in Springfield, Missouri. After graduation in 1956, Falwell returned to Lynchburg and started the only church he has ever pastored, Thomas Road Baptist Church. With a congregation hovering around twenty thousand, Falwell's is now one of the five largest churches in the country.

During the 1960s and early 1970s, Falwell's ministry followed a pattern familiar to students of Fundamentalism. Adopting methods developed and perfected by some other pastors in the Bible Baptist Association who had built huge churches, Falwell's congregation grew enormously. Typical of such churches, the sermons were usually evangelistic in nature. The plan of salvation was explained, sinners were exhorted to be saved, and many were. Churches in this mold tended to slight more serious Bible study that supported Christian growth. Certainly, there was no thought in those early days of devoting any sermon to some social or political issue. The discovery of the social implications of the Christian gospel was still several years away. Falwell now admits being critical in the 1960s and early 1970s of religious leaders who mixed religion and politics. He also admits that he was wrong.

The 1970s was a decade of change in America. Whether

America was ever in truth "a Christian nation," it rapidly began to be much less so during the seventies. The growing tide of immorality, the growing challenge of Secular Humanism, and, above all, the growing contempt for human life and values, as reflected in the aftermath of the *Roe v. Wade* decision, helped Falwell to see that no conscientious Christian could remain silent at such a time.

Falwell's negative image results not only from the way he and his views are caricatured, but also from the unpopularity of some of his causes. Many of Falwell's enemies misrepresent him as a closed-minded zealot who is anxious to reinstitute the Inquisition. But any fair critic who has watched Falwell in debate has to admit that the man is sincere and has somehow mastered the facts and arguments required to present his cause in a plausible way. Falwell has debated the cases he represents in some of the most hostile settings possible, including Harvard and Oxford Universities. Frequently, people who entered such debates convinced that the stereotype of Falwell so often presented in the press was true left thinking that just possibly the upstart fundamentalist might have won the debate.

In 1979, Falwell and four other conservative clergymen—Tim LaHaye, Greg Dixon, Charles Stanley, and D. James Kennedy—joined forces to found Moral Majority.[1] In January of 1986, Falwell announced that Moral Majority was being absorbed into a larger and more comprehensive organization to be called the Liberty Federation, which would address political as well as moral issues. Because the Moral Majority label induced strong negative feelings in so many people, and because the goals of Moral Majority were so widely misunderstood, it was thought that the new name would help the organization avoid much of the prejudice associated with the old label. Representatives of Moral Majority often did their organization a disservice by stating their goals in ways that made them appear enemies of a pluralistic society. This image was often enhanced by the ill-considered actions of extremists and zealots, whose understanding of a democratic society and of the organization's goals were wanting. Falwell has made it plain that none of the leaders of Moral Majority are enemies of a free, open, and pluralistic society. But they are enemies of a liberal and humanistic intolerance toward traditional religious and moral values that would exclude the values of the majority of Americans from public life. Falwell does not want an America in which 100 percent of the Supreme Court, the Congress, and the president are fundamentalists. Nor, as he has recently told some Jewish audiences, is he striving to turn America into a "Christian" nation. The values he wants to help restore to America are the moral and religious values of the Judeo-Christian tradition. Falwell's goals for America differ little from the aspirations of many mainline Protestants, Roman Catholics, and Jews who believe that America is heading in the wrong direction morally and religiously.[2]

Carl F. H. Henry

While Carl F. H. Henry's name is not nearly so familiar to the general public as that of Billy Graham or Jerry Falwell, he has probably had more influence on the development of contemporary Evangelicalism than anyone, save Graham. Without question, Carl Henry is the foremost evangelical theologian of the twentieth century.

Born in 1913, Henry was not converted until after he had begun a career in journalism. He then entered Wheaton College, where, in the late 1930s, he received both bachelor's and master's degrees. Henry went on to earn two doctorates, a Th.D. from Northern Baptist Theological Seminary and a Ph.D. from Boston University. He was undoubtedly the intellectual leader of the evangelical movement that began in the late 1940s.

When Fuller Theological Seminary was started in the late

1940s, Henry was a member of the founding faculty. During this time, he published the most influential of his early books, *The Uneasy Conscience of Modern Fundamentalism*, in which he chided fundamentalists for their inattention to social issues. In 1956, Henry left Fuller to become the founding editor of *Christianity Today*. After leaving the journal in 1968, Henry taught at such schools as Eastern Baptist Seminary, Trinity Evangelical Divinity School, Calvin Theological Seminary, and Hillsdale College. He also served as Lecturer-at-Large for World Vision, a Christian relief organization. This position gave him numerous opportunities to share his understanding of evangelical theology in Third-World nations.

Henry is the author or editor of more than thirty books. The culmination of his publishing activity is his massive six-volume work *God, Revelation and Authority*.[3] According to Henry, the time has come to be done with nebulous views of the Christian God and with skepticism about either humankind's ability to attain knowledge about God or God's ability to communicate truth. In Henry's view, the entire enterprise of Christian theology must be grounded on God's self-revelation. Henry points out that modern humanity exists in a cultural milieu pervaded by irrationalism and suspicion about all claims to absolute truth. Secular humanity often disparages Christianity as irrational. But the truth is that revealed religion and the recovery of the respect for reason must go together. Christian theology is not and cannot be opposed to reason and logic. Revealed religion is possible because God has made humankind in his image and has given him a rational ability to perceive the truth that God has revealed.[4]

Carl Henry represents the very best of evangelical scholarship over a period of some forty years. He has championed the twin causes of orthodoxy and orthopraxis, fidelity to the theological concerns of historic Christianity and concern for the social implications of that faith.

Francis Schaeffer

Francis Schaeffer was born in Germantown, Pennsylvania in 1912. Although a Presbyterian, Schaeffer was attracted to a dispensational and separatist type of Fundamentalism from about 1936 through the late 1940s. During much of this time, Shaeffer was closely associated with Carl McIntyre, the leader of the International Council of Christian Churches, a small fundamentalist competitor to the World Council of Churches. In 1948, Schaeffer and his family traveled to Switzerland as missionaries. In the early 1950s, after breaking with McIntyre several years before, Schaeffer and his wife began a ministry in Switzerland that would eventually become the retreat known as L'Abri. Gradually, word began to spread that there was a man at L'Abri who could help people who had intellectual problems regarding Christianity. Through years of discussion, study, and counseling, Schaeffer developed an approach to the interrelationship between Christianity and culture that led growing numbers of individuals to study at L'Abri.

During the 1960s, some of Schaeffer's lectures to American college students were taped and then turned into the small books that first brought him national attention. These first books included *The God Who Is There* and *Escape from Reason*.[5] The steady stream of books that followed helped Schaeffer acquire a large following among college students and educated adults. Through the early 1970s, his books dealt with such traditional evangelical concerns as apologetics (the intellectual defense of the faith), the formulation of a Christian world view, and the relations between Christianity and culture. Academic specialists in the fields Schaeffer treated often complained about the allegedly superficial and inaccurate nature of many of his claims. Schaeffer himself knew when such criticisms were justified. He replied that he was really just an evangelist who was attempting to get a public that was seldom interested in thinking very deeply to begin reflecting about such things as philosophy and art. His purpose was to get people to begin the process of thinking; after they had started to think about philosophy, they could turn to philosophers for the full account.

A major shift in Schaeffer's work became evident in 1976 with the publication of a book about the history of Western culture from a Christian perspective. Entitled *How Should We Then Live?*,[6] the book was accompanied by a series of films, featuring Schaeffer, that were shown widely around the country. In 1979, he helped to mobilize evangelical opposition to abortion-on-demand with his book *Whatever Happened to the Human Race?*, co-authored with Dr. C. Everett Koop, a nationally known surgeon who would become Surgeon General of the United States during the Reagan administration.[7] Schaeffer died of cancer in May, 1984.

While Schaeffer's enormous influence on Evangelicalism is undoubtedly due to his lectures, films, and books (which have sold more than three million copies world-wide), his most important accomplishment may have taken place behind the scenes. Some have suggested that Schaeffer was the catalyst that turned world-denying fundamentalists like Jerry Falwell and Tim LaHaye into social activists determined to reclaim their culture for Christ. More than anything else, Schaeffer's influence may have led conservative Evangelicalism to embark on a crusade to turn America around. Not everyone will appreciate this fact, of course, but it is an amazing tribute to the difference that one man can make.[8]

Pat Robertson

Marion G. ("Pat") Robertson, son of a long-time Democratic United States Senator, was born in Virginia in 1930. Robertson, himself, was a life-long Democrat until recently, when he switched parties and announced that he was considering a run for the Republican presidential nomination.

Following graduation from Washington and Lee University in 1950, Robertson completed a law degree at Yale in 1955 and a Master of Divinity degree from New York Theological Seminary in 1959. In 1961, he started the nation's first Christian television station (WYAH) in Portsmouth, Virginia. In the years following, he added other television stations (which he has since sold) and began the television program known as "700 Club."

With the expansion of cable television and the technical advances made possible by television satellites, Robertson's work expanded into what is now the Christian Broadcasting Network (CBN). More than thirty-two hundred cable systems carry CBN and provide it with access to more than thirty million homes twenty-four hours a day. In addition, Robertson's "700 Club" is available on one hundred fifty regular television stations. CBN programming is available in twenty-two countries; Robertson has expanded CBN into what amounts to a fourth television network.

In 1977, Robertson founded CBN University in Virginia Beach, Virginia. The university offers graduate level programs in religion, journalism, public affairs, and law. CBN University has recently taken over operation of the law school of Oral Roberts University and has moved it to the Virginia Beach campus.

Robertson's vast audience, the wide appeal of his "700 Club," and his effective, but low-key, presentation may make him the most influential representative of New Pentecostalism in the country. Non-pentecostal evangelicals appreciate the fact that he places his primary emphasis upon the importance of conversion.

C. S. Lewis

Few evangelicals would challenge the inclusion of British evangelical Lewis in this brief list of representative evangelicals. Clive Staples Lewis belongs in this list, most would agree, because of the enormous influence his writings have had on mainstream Evangelicalism. During the 1940s and 1950s when anti-intellectualism was such an unfortunate trait of much American conservatism, exposure to Lewis' books led many evangelicals into their first serious reflection about ethics, theology, and apologetics.

Lewis was born in Belfast, Northern Ireland, in 1898. After being wounded near the end of World War I, he completed his education at University College, Oxford. Between 1925 and 1954, Lewis was a Fellow in English Language and Literature at Magdalen College, Oxford.

A nominal Anglican in his youth, Lewis had become an atheist. This changed, however, in 1929 when he became persuaded that God exists and that theism is true. His actual conversion to Christianity followed soon after. Lewis began to publish his reflections on religious subjects that proved so popular in the late 1930s and early 1940s. His study of the problem of evil, *The Problem of Pain*, was published in England in 1940. This was followed in 1941 by his imaginative series of letters between a senior and an apprentice demon, *The Screwtape Letters*. During the war years, he gave a series of broadcast talks over the B.B.C. that were eventually combined and published under the title *Mere Christianity*. His defense of the possibility of miracles appeared as *Miracles: A Preliminary Study*. The first of his charming theological allegories in the Narnia series, *The Lion, the Witch and the Wardrobe*, was published in 1950.[9]

As Lewis' many fans know only too well, this list of his books is far from complete, but these were the major works that helped so many who had become indifferent to Christian claims to reexamine their relationship to the historic faith Lewis called "mere Christianity." Especially important to this study of Evangelicalism is the fact that Lewis' books were available at a time when evangelical scholars were publishing little or nothing in these areas. Lewis' writings helped to fill the breach until evangelical publishing finally hit its stride.

One of the passages for which Lewis is best remembered was his demonstration of how simple-minded unitarianism is. According to Lewis, the belief that Jesus was just a good man, albeit a great moral teacher, contradicts everything we know about Jesus. Someone who was just a *good* man could never have done the things and said the things that Jesus did. Jesus claimed to be God; he claimed to have created the world; he said that he would one day judge all human beings for their sins; he allowed people to worship him as God; he claimed to have the power to forgive sins. Now, Lewis said, it simply does not make sense to continue to regard someone like this as a good man. Either Jesus was not good, or he was not simply human. In a passage that has become classic, Lewis hammers home the logical conclusion:

> I am trying here to prevent anyone saying the really foolish thing that people often say about Him: "I'm ready to accept Jesus as a great moral teacher, but I don't accept His claim to be God." That is the one thing we must not say. A man who was merely a man and said the sort of things Jesus said would not be a great moral teacher. He would either be a lunatic—on a level with the man who says he is a poached egg—or else he would be the Devil of Hell. You must make your choice. Either this man was, and is, the Son of God: or else a madman or something worse. You can shut Him up for a fool, you can spit at Him and kill Him as a demon; or you can fall at His feet and call Him Lord and God. But let us not come with any patronising nonsense about His being a great human teacher. He has not left that open to us. He did not intend to.[10]

In 1955, Lewis accepted the position of Professor of Medieval and Renaissance Literature at Magdalen College, Cambridge. His marriage to an American in 1956 was quickly followed by the discovery that she was suffering from a terminal case of cancer. After a remarkable remission of the cancer that lasted for several years, Lewis' wife died in 1960. Lewis, himself, died on November 22, 1963, the same day that John F. Kennedy was assassinated.

Conclusion

If this list of representative evangelicals could be expanded, it would include such names as J. Gresham Machen, Harold John Ockenga, Gordon H. Clark, Cornelius Van Til, Edward John Carnell, Kenneth Kantzer, J. Oliver Buswell, Jr., John Stott, James Packer, and Charles Colson—to name but a very few. Future generations of evangelicals will be able to see much further because of the work of men such as these.

CHAPTER EIGHT

Evangelical Pressure Points

Evangelicalism is not a monolithic movement. Its diversity is reflected in disagreements that divide evangelicals into fundamentalists, pentecostals, and mainstream evangelicals; into Calvinists and Arminians; into different views of the sacraments and church polity; hence, into different denominational fellowships. But evangelicals also part company on many of the same complex social and cultural issues that divide the societies to which they belong. This chapter will take note of a number of areas in which evangelical disagreements exist. In a few instances, the question is so important and the divisions so deep that it sometimes looks as though evangelicals are standing on the brink of a civil war. In keeping with the general nature of this book, it is not the purpose of this chapter to offer solutions to these problems; rather it is to identify them and to direct the reader to some literature that can serve as the starting point for a more detailed examination of the issue.

The divisions among contemporary evangelicals are occurring along two major fault lines. The first concerns conflicting evangelical views about the Bible. The second concerns important disagreements about the interpretation of the Bible and its application to some of the most pressing social and cultural issues of the day.

The Battle for the Bible

Harold Lindsell, at the time editor of *Christianity Today*, drew attention to evangelical dissension over Scripture in a 1976 book entitled *The Battle for the Bible*.[1] According to Lindsell, scores of professed evangelicals, holding positions of trust and responsibility at evangelical institutions, had effectively abandoned key elements of the evangelical view of Scripture. Given the widespread looseness with regard to the Bible, it was only a matter of time, Lindsell argued, until these institutions, individuals, or those who followed them, would emulate the religious liberals of earlier in this century and abandon other central doctrines. In fact, Lindsell maintained, this was already occurring in the colleges and seminaries of his own denomination, the Southern Baptist Convention. Equally shocking to many were Lindsell's claims about liberal inroads at Fuller Theological Seminary, where Lindsell, along with Carl Henry, had been a professor. The central focus of Lindsell's claim was the doctrine of biblical inerrancy, the belief that Scripture contains no errors.

Carl Henry, himself a firm advocate of inerrancy, agreed with Lindsell that the doctrine of biblical inerrancy was in fact being denied in a number of institutions that were supposed to be evangelical. But Henry disagreed with Lindsell's insistence that the doctrine of inerrancy was the litmus test of being a true evangelical. However much Henry regretted the fact that some evangelicals were wavering on the doctrine of inerrancy, he was not quite ready—on that count alone—to dismiss them from the evangelical camp.[2]

On another front, the battle for the Bible reflected differing evangelical attitudes toward the use of biblical criticism. Several years ago, Robert Gundry, a professor of New Testament at Westmont College, was dropped from the membership of the Evangelical Theological Society because of certain conclusions he reached regarding the Gospel of

Matthew through his use of redaction criticism. Even though Gundry insisted on his commitment to biblical inerrancy, the society found his conclusions inconsistent with his professedly high view of Scripture and expelled him. More recently, a New Testament scholar at Gordon-Conwell Theological Seminary was let go for his own conclusions about certain passages in the Gospels that seemed dictated by his critical methodology. These were especially painful episodes since both men are respected evangelicals. Hard-line believers in inerrancy argue that it is essential for evangelicals to draw the line and to hold it. These same hard-liners say that because the inerrancy cause has already been lost at some evangelical institutions, it is only a matter of time before the cancer of liberalism affects the entire school. Opponents of the hard-liners have replied that inerrancy is a relatively new doctrine in the history of Christian thought. In their view, it is still possible to hold a reverent and high view of Scripture without abandoning the tools of biblical criticism or without subscribing to biblical inerrancy.

Some observers of the dispute between the friends and critics of biblical inerrancy have wondered if some of the disagreement may not result from confusion about what the doctrine of inerrancy means. Perhaps, they suggest, opponents of inerrancy are rejecting inerrancy doctrine A when, in fact, the inerrantists are actually defending doctrine B. To eliminate, or at least ease this possibility, a number of inerrantists got together in the late 1970s and issued what has become known as "The Chicago Statement on Biblical Inerrancy."[3] The Chicago Statement affirmed the full truthfulness of Scripture: "Being wholly and verbally God-given, Scripture is without error or fault in all its teaching, no less in what it states about God's acts in creation, about the events of world history, and about its own literary origins under God, than in its witness to God's saving grace in individual lives."[4]

This statement makes two points: (1) all of the Bible is

truthful in what it teaches, and (2) the Bible is true even when it touches on such matters as history that have nothing to do with salvation. This last point was a slap at people who hold a position known as "limited inerrancy." For a limited inerrantist, the Bible is inerrant in what it "teaches," but its teaching is limited to matters relating to human salvation. Therefore, non-salvational biblical statements about some matters of history, geography, or science may contain errors. But since this should not be included within the sphere of biblical *teaching*, the presence of such errors should create no great difficulties for those who hold a high view of Scripture.

The authors of the Chicago statement disagreed. "We deny," they wrote, "that Biblical infallibility and inerrancy are limited to spiritual, religious or redemptive themes, exclusive of assertions in the fields of history and science."[5] Such a stance imposes the task of reconciling apparent contradictions within Scripture and apparent inconsistencies between statements in the Bible and evidence from extra-biblical sources. This challenge is welcomed by inerrantists.

Some critics of inerrancy make sweeping claims about hundreds of alleged discrepancies in the Bible. Responding to one such claim, Carl Henry countered by writing:

> Such extravagant claims are possible only if one holds that literary differences of style and vocabulary are logical contradictions. . . . The alleged errors that [James] Barr specifically adduces add nothing to the list that competent scholars have previously acknowledged and grappled with; his agenda contains little more than one will find in pamphlets from the Rationalist Press and the writings of Tom Paine; most evangelical scholars, in fact, would even add a few more.[6]

An important first step in any sensible approach to the inerrancy question is distinguishing errors in the text of the Bible that have usually resulted from the mistakes of early copyists from the really serious problem of alleged errors and contradictions in the original writings, the so-called autographs. The Chicago Statement specifically denies "that inerrancy is negated by Biblical phenomena such as a lack of modern technical precision, irregularities of grammar or spelling, observational descriptions of nature, the reporting of falsehoods, the use of hyperbole and round numbers, the topical arrangement of metrical, variant selections of material in parallel accounts, or the use of free citations."[7]

Evangelical inerrantists do not insist that multiple accounts of the same event should use the same words in their descriptions or that all quotations of earlier writings be verbally exact (biblical writers often quoted from memory) or that biblical statements about natural phenomena should be scientifically accurate. In most cases, the Bible refers to natural phenomena in language that is popular rather than scientific. This is the same thing modern men and women do when they refer to the rising and setting of the sun. But evangelicals do object to the instant assumption of many biblical critics that every difficulty in the Bible should be viewed as an error.

It is important to remember that the Bible was written in patterns of thought that represent an Oriental milieu, often differing from our own. Like any written work, the Bible should be judged in terms of its faithfulness to its intended purpose. For this reason, the writers of the Chicago Statement "deny that it is proper to evaluate Scripture according to standards of truth and error that are alien to its usage or purpose."[8]

Have the defenders of inerrancy answered all of the challenges? Have they resolved all of the problems? Carl Henry admits that they have not.[9] But, Henry counters, while the list of alleged errors in the Bible has grown shorter over the years, the list of the errors made by critics of Scripture grows longer. While the inerrancy case is not helped by simply ignoring the problems, Henry declares, the history of the attack on inerrancy provides grounds for optimism that future discoveries will resolve the remaining difficulties.

The critically important question is whether evangelical scholars approach the Bible with the conviction that it is wholly trustworthy and reliable and that all of its teaching is the word of the God, who cannot lie.

Putting the issue of inerrancy aside, we find that a number of other criticisms of Evangelicalism's high view of Scripture are based on misunderstandings or misrepresentations of what evangelicals actually believe. For example, evangelicals are often ridiculed as practicing bibliolatry. This charge is a canard and is unworthy of any responsible critic of Evangelicalism. Evangelicals certainly know the difference between worshiping the Bible and worshiping the God of the Bible. Nor do evangelicals deny the fact that Scripture contains an important human element. Even though God guided the inspired writers by his Holy Spirit so that their words convey the meaning that God intended, the biblical writings still reflect the culture, the personal backgrounds, the personalities, and the distinctive vocabularies of the human authors. Paul's vocabulary and writing style are distinct, for example, from Luke's. The Bible was not a product of a mechanical kind of dictation, nor does divine inspiration preclude the use of poetry and other non-literal uses of language. In reading the Bible,

> history must be treated as history, poetry as poetry, hyperbole and metaphor as hyperbole and metaphor, generalization and approximation as what they are, and so forth. Differences between literary conventions in Bible times and in our time must also be observed: since, for instance nonchronological narration and imprecise citation were conventional and acceptable and violated no expectations in those days, we must not regard these things as faults when we find them in Bible writers. When total precision of a particular kind was not expected nor aimed at, it is no error not to have achieved it.

Scripture is inerrant, not in the sense of being absolutely precise by modern standards, but in the sense of making good its claims and achieving that measure of focused truth at which its authors aimed.[10]

The evangelical's high view of Scripture is not necessarily incompatible with with the use of biblical criticism. As evangelical scholar George Ladd explained: "To be a critic means merely to ask questions about the authorship, date, place, sources, purpose, and so on, of any ancient literary work. The opposite of a properly "critical" approach to the study of the Bible is, therefore, an unthinking, unquestioning acceptance of tradition. To be non-critical means simply to ignore altogether the historical dimension of the Bible and to view it as a magical book."[11]

The evangelical use of biblical criticism differs from the non-evangelical in several ways. First, evangelicals are conscious and critical of the extent to which naturalistic presuppositions dictate many of the conclusions to which non-evangelical biblical critics are led. As Carl Henry observes, "What is objectionable is not historical-critical method, but rather the alien presuppositions to which neo-Protestants subject it. Combination of the method with an antisupernaturalistic bias reflects not a requirement of the method but a prejudice of the historian."[12] More radical practitioners of biblical criticism have often decided their view of the Bible before starting their critical investigations. The results of much liberal criticism often appear to be dictated more by theological and philosophical prejudices than by objective analysis.

Second, liberal and evangelical biblical critics often approach their task from different perspectives. "The liberal tends to approach the task [of biblical criticism] from the scientific side; criticism is a given, and the liberal looks for the religious values still to be found in the Bible despite its human and historic conditioning. The evangelical approaches from the biblical side; the authority of Scripture is given, and the question is how criticism can help to understand it."[13]

This characteristic of the evangelical approach results from the view of Jesus Christ and the relationship that exists between the authority of Christ and the authority of the Bible. Because evangelicals believe that Jesus Christ speaks with divine authority, his view on any subject, including the Bible, becomes normative for the Christian. Evangelicals challenge all views of the Bible that conflict with Jesus' own understanding of it as inspired and authoritative.[14]

Even when evangelicals agree about the authority of the Bible and its content, an additional set of problems arises in connection with the question: *What does the Bible mean?*

> The infallibility and inerrancy of biblical teaching does not, however, guarantee the infallibility and inerrancy of any interpretation, or interpreter, of that teaching; nor does the recognition of its qualities as the word of God in any way prejudge the issue as to what Scripture does, in fact, assert. This can be determined only by careful Bible study.[15]

The important issues connected with the interpretation of the biblical text are dealt with by the branch of theology known as *hermeneutics.* Hermeneutics is an extremely complex subject to which evangelical scholars are devoting much attention.[16] To some extent, these investigations of hermeneutics offer answers to a very difficult question: If God has given Christians an inspired Bible, why do they have so much difficulty reaching agreement on what the Bible says?

But evangelical disagreements over complex social issues reflect more than difficulties in determining the meaning of the biblical text. They also mirror the problems that conscientious people face when they grapple with difficult moral problems and attempt to apply biblical truth to complicated and perplexing issues that have entered the arena of public debate only in this century.

The Battle Over Social Issues

Evangelicals disagree over most of the same social and moral issues that divide thinking people in the Western nations—abortion, feminism, homosexuality, national defense, nuclear disarmament, Central America—as well as the interlocking network of issues and problems that divide people into liberals and conservatives.[17] There is at least one good side to all these disagreements. If anyone is attracted to Evangelicalism for religious reasons, but repelled by what he or she believes is *the* evangelical position on an issue, it may help that person to realize that the critically important things are the Lordship of Christ and conversion and submission to the authority of God's Word. When evangelicals argue about an issue, they use the same tools of evidence, argument, and inference that non-evangelicals use. The major difference is their concern to square their convictions with the Word of God. Obviously, this can often be difficult enough to allow for some flexibility within the evangelical family. When the issue is important enough and when convictions are strong enough, the arguments can get fairly heated. In other words, becoming an evangelical does not necessarily commit one in advance to a particular social and political agenda.

The final section of this chapter will examine two areas in which evangelical disagreement exists. They are the question of abortion and the dispute over political and economic issues dividing evangelicals into liberals and conservatives.

Evangelical involvement in the abortion debate is well-known. Evangelical Francis Schaeffer captured the spirit of millions of evangelicals when he and co-author C. Everett Koop began their book, *Whatever Happened to the Human Race?* with the words: "Cultures can be judged in many ways, but eventually every nation in every age must be judged by this test: *how did it treat people?* Each generation, each wave of humanity, evaluates its predecessors on this basis. The final measure of mankind's humanity is how humanely people treat one another."[18]

The nations of the world are justified in condemning Nazi Germany. The Holocaust that killed six million Jews occurred because, in that nation, the "unthinkable" had become "thinkable." Something similar has happened in America that continues to condemn the unthinkable evil of the Holocaust.

> What we regard as thinkable and unthinkable about how we treat human life has changed drastically in the West. For centuries Western culture has regarded human life and the quality of the life of the individual as special. It has been common to speak of "the sanctity of human life." Until recently in our own century, with some notable and sorry exceptions, human beings have generally been regarded as special, unique, and nonexpendable. But in one short generation we have moved from a generally high view of life to a very low one.[19]

For Schaeffer, this shift in values reflects, perhaps better than anything else, the fact that our society has abandoned its Judeo-Christian base for a humanistic one that "puts man rather than God at the center of all things."[20] Americans are part of a culture that now terminates about a million and a half fetuses a year. By the end of 1986 approximately twenty million abortions will have been performed in America alone since the *Roe v. Wade* decision of 1973. If one believes that a fetus is a human being, one does not have to be an evangelical to feel outrage at this carnage and to feel shame over what it reveals about the moral tone of America.

Of course, many Americans deny the humanity of the fetus. The positions of the combatants in this dispute are well-known. Therefore, no attempt will be made to summarize the various arguments. The issue of abortion-on-demand must be mentioned because of its importance in leading millions of conservative Protestants, who for decades had turned away from their culture and social problems, into becoming social activists. Innocent and defenseless human beings were being slaughtered by the millions with the consent of the nation's courts, they believed. For Christians to remain silent in the face of this American Holocaust was unthinkable.

The opening salvos in what has become an increasingly serious dispute between social liberals and conservatives within Evangelicalism were fired by members of the evangelical Left. A number of books published around 1970 attacked what was called an uncritical alliance between the religious and political Right.[21] While many politically conservative evangelicals recognized the legitimacy of some claims in these books, they were also disturbed by rather obvious weaknesses. For one thing, conservatives noticed, the authors of the books seemed totally unfamiliar with the writings of responsible representatives of the conservative mainstream who had disassociated their movement from racists and other extremists who were not conservative at all. In some cases, books by the evangelical Left reflected no awareness of the nature of mainstream conservatism. Moreover, conservative evangelicals wondered if the spokespersons for the evangelical Left were not simply replacing an uncritical alliance with "the Right" with an equally uncritical alliance with "the Left." A third concern is related to the Left's apparent arrogance and intolerance toward Christians who held any view of society that differed from theirs. They seemed to be saying that no sincere and informed evangelical should have anything to do with that evil system known as conservatism. "Come out from them and be separate, says the Lord" (II Corinthians 6:17). A new kind of separatism had been born.

The attacks took a new turn in the mid-1970s when

members of the evangelical Left took the additional step of equating political conservatism with selfish materialism and a callous indifference to the plight of the poor. It had now become something of a sin to vote for a candidate like Ronald Reagan. On a number of evangelical campuses, political conservatism was equated with subchristian and even unchristian attitudes toward the poor. By the early 1980s, a number of evangelicals had moved far beyond more traditional forms of American liberalism toward the kind of Christian Marxism being advocated by representatives of liberation theology. Extremists within the evangelical Left began to promote the Marxist claim that all poverty results from oppression. And when this poverty occurs in Third World nations, their argument continued, the obvious cause must be the capitalist nations of the West, the preeminent culprit being the United States. America, these evangelicals suggested, was precisely what the leaders of Iran said it was— "The Great Satan." *Sojourners* magazine appeared to blame the United States for every major evil in the world, including the murder of millions of Cambodians by communists, the Soviet invasion of Afghanistan, and the Soviet's shooting down of a Korean airliner.[22] Some careful readers of *Sojourners* found it increasingly difficult to find any evangelical content in the magazine. The gospel, it appeared, had become secondary. What the magazine was most interested in doing, critics complained, was promoting its radical political causes.[23]

Varieties of Marxist thought have become deeply entrenched on several major evangelical campuses. Some evangelical sociologists criticize their society from a Marxist perspective, while some evangelical economics departments present socialism as the only option for thinking Christians.

Because some of the same trends were occurring within Roman Catholicism, the earliest challenges to the growing merger of Christian social thought with political and economic collectivism came from Roman Catholic scholars like Michael Novak.[24] The first serious response from an evangelical seems to have been a 1979 article in *Christianity Today* that was followed by several other books and articles.[25] In this conservative response, several points were made: (1) It is not enough for evangelicals simply to *talk* about helping the poor. Their compassion for the poor must be wedded to a sound economics so that their efforts will help rather than harm the poor. (2) Because of problems inherent in collectivist approaches to economics, the programs supported by the evangelical Left have actually had a devastating effect on the poor. According to several recent studies, antipoverty programs in the United States have in fact increased poverty.[26] Based on evidence available from two decades of Great Society programs, members of the evangelical Left have been promoting programs that have injured the poor. According to economist James Gwartney of Florida State University:

> Seeking to promote the welfare of the poor, the disadvantaged, the unemployed, and the misfortunate, well-meaning citizens (including a good many evangelical Christians) have inadvertently supported forms of economic organization that have promoted the precise outcomes they sought to alleviate. For too long, socially concerned Christians have measured policies by the intentions of their advocates, rather than the predictable effectiveness of the programs. Put simply, in our haste to do something constructive, we have not thought very seriously about the impact, particularly in the long-run, of alternative policies on the well-being of the intended beneficiaries.[27]

Other spokespersons for a less radical evangelical position on economics and society have begun to speak out. Writing in a well-received book entitled *Idols for Destruction*, Herbert Schlossberg could find little in the allegedly prophetic voice of the Christian Left save constant bellyaching without any necessity for discrimination, reason, or knowledge. In general, the radical Christian left has been a shrill scream, indiscriminately labeling everything it dislikes as idolatrous. . . . Moreover, its hasty identification with the prophetic writings [of the Old Testament] that denounce those who oppress the poor lead it to divinize the poor and to cooperate with the policies of social democracy that turn poverty into a permanent condition. Imposing helplessness on poor people, it works to ensure the triumph of . . . policies that condemn the poor to perpetual dependency. Having lost the power of discrimination, this type of radicalism mindlessly associates itself with any expression of antiestablishment feeling and so substitutes a shabby anti-Americanism for a truly radical gospel.[28]

While these were harsh words, they were applauded by many evangelical moderates. Ken Myers, the respected former editor of *Eternity* magazine, wonders "why some Evangelicals seem to be eager to bear a sputtering torch, to become the eager champions of programs and perspectives on American political and social life that have . . . come to seem either foolish or at least open to serious debate. Specifically, I have been disheartened to see a replica of the mentality of the Sixties emerge in nominally Evangelical circles. Such a mentality expresses to one degree or another the belief that America is the chief cause of suffering and evil in the world, that Western culture has no redeeming or redeemable values, and that the malignancies of Marxist-Leninist regimes are purely a natural reaction to American bellicosity."[29]

Myers finds other features of the evangelical fascination with sixties-style radicalism worthy of comment:

It is most fascinating that such a vision of the world should re-emerge at precisely the time when many of those who, not long ago believed such things and preached revolution on behalf of their beliefs, are now repudiating them, and adopting a stance much more consistent with the liberal tradition in America. That tradition has been unapologetically pro-democratic and anti-communist, and boasts a long list of respected adherents, many of them prominent intellectuals. Today, such a tradition is regaining credibility in such places as the pages of *The New Republic* and *The Partisan Review*. But, irony of ironies, the stance of historical American liberalism is regarded as reactionary and uninformed in many Evangelical circles.[30]

It is interesting to note that the most significant moves toward dialogue and reconciliation among the combatants have been initiated by conservatives. Lutheran theologian Richard John Neuhaus, of The Center on Religion and Society (a branch of the conservative Rockford Foundation), recently convened a group of some twenty evangelical liberals and conservatives to discuss their differences. The conservative side was represented by Tim LaHaye and Jerry Falwell associate Ed Dobson. The evangelical Left was represented by Ronald Sider, author of *Rich Christians in an Age of Hunger*,[31] and Calvin College philosopher Nicholas Wolterstorff, an editor of *The Reformed Journal*. The meeting helped to dispell misunderstandings on all sides. Similar meetings that focus on economic questions have been convened by the Political Economy Research Center under support from the conservative Liberty Fund. Observers at these meetings agree that Evangelicalism needs more of this kind of face to face dialogue.

Conclusion

It would be unfortunate if the problems and divisions of Evangelicalism that have been noted in this chapter should divert attention away from its many positive features. In one sense, this evangelical disagreement serves as evidence for the fact that when someone becomes an evangelical, he or she does not surrender the right to think reflectively about controversial issues and disagree with others who share a commitment to Jesus Christ. Whatever problems Evangelicalism may seem to face, boredom does not seem to be one of them. As a matter of fact, so far as religion in America is concerned, Evangelicalism is, to use a non-religious colloquialism, "where all the action is."

In conclusion, it may be helpful to put the more serious evangelical disagreements aside and remember once again what being an evangelical is all about. As one writer puts it, the word *evangelical* refers "to Christians of whatever denomination who are determined to rest their faith and religious practice on the authority of the Bible; who believe that the New Testament promises eternal life through a moral transforming experience of the Holy Spirit that Jesus described to Nicodemus as being "born again"; and who are, for these reasons, intensely committed to missionary work ("evangelism"), both in their own towns and neighborhoods and around the world."[32] These are the truly important features of Evangelicalism.

Evangelicalism heralds good news for the whole man and for the whole world. It proffers the prospect of the self-made whole and the world turned right-side up. It is not an "instant cure" since it calls for personal decision, and the Bible warns that some will refuse to come to terms with God and thus face final judgment. But for the sin-sick soul and a sin-warped society, no message holds more promise and power than does the life-transforming message of Jesus Christ.

1. The Evangelical Resurgence

1. Richard G. Hutcheson, Jr., *Mainline Churches and the Evangelicals* (Atlanta: John Knox Press, 1981), p. 39.

2. Ibid., p. 43.

3. Ibid., p. 8.

2. Who Are the Evangelicals?

1. As the Apostle Paul explained in I Corinthians 15:3-4, the gospel includes—at the minimum—a proper understanding of what Jesus Christ did for human beings through his death and resurrection.

2. James I. Packer, *Fundamentalism and the Word of God* (Grand Rapids: Eerdmans, 1958), 22. James I. Packer is one of several British evangelicals who have come to have a significant influence in America. Packer, who received his B.A., M.A., and Ph.D. degrees from Oxford University, is a member of the Church of England. While teaching in England during the 1960s and 1970s, he authored several books that have been widely used in the United States. For several years, he has taught theology at Regent College in Vancouver, British Columbia. He lectures widely across the United States.

3. See William G. McLoughlin, ed., *The American Evangelicals, 1800-1900: An Anthology* (New York: Peter Smith 1968), 1, pp. 30-31.

4. Robert E. Webber, *Common Roots: A Call to Evangelical Maturity* (Grand Rapids: Zondervan, 1982), p. 30.

5. At the risk of making the discussion of evangelical subcultures even more complicated, an important qualification must be added. The evangelical mainstream also includes some confessional, or reformed, denominations that emphasize the importance of the Christian family in the birth and nurture of Christian faith. Large numbers of people, in such denominations as the Christian Reformed Church, clearly base all of their hope for eternal life upon the death and resurrection of Christ, in spite of the fact that many of them cannot point to a specific experience of conversion.

6. See Richard G. Hutcheson, Jr., *Mainline Churches and the Evangelicals* (Atlanta: John Knox Press, 1981), pp. 80-81.

7. For an example of such criticism, see Lloyd Billingsley, *The Generation That Knew Not Josef* (Portland: Multnomah Press, 1985).

3. Evangelical Roots

1. William Hordern, *A Layman's Guide to Protestant Theology*, revised ed. (New York: Macmillan, 1968), p. 1.

2. For more on this, consult Ronald Nash, *The Concept of God* (Grand Rapids: Zondervan, 1983) and Ronald Nash, ed., *Process Theology* (Grand Rapids: Baker Book House, 1987).

3. The Nicene Creed grew out of the work of the Council of Nicaea (A.D. 325) and the Council of Constantinople (A.D. 381). It received official acceptance at the Council of Chalcedon in A.D. 451. It is Christianity's oldest theological statement.

4. The Nicene Creed settled the question of the relationship between Jesus Christ, God the Son, and God the Father. But it left unanswered the relation between Jesus' human nature and his divine nature. If we say, with the Nicene Creed, that Jesus was fully God, what should Christians believe about Jesus' humanity? Was he fully human? Was he simply God masquerading as a human being? The essence of the Chalcedonian doctrine is that Jesus possessed two natures in one person. While the person of Jesus was undivided, this one person possessed, as a result of the incarnation, two natures: one divine and one human. Jesus was fully God *and* fully human. He was the God-man. When dealing with the person of Jesus and his divine and human natures, it is important that we neither divide the person of Jesus nor confuse the two natures.

5. John Stott, *Basic Christianity* (Grand Rapids: Eerdmans, 1957), 22. John Stott, former rector of All Souls' Church in London, is another evangelical in the Church of England who has had a significant impact on American evangelicals through his writings and lectures.

6. For a discussion of liberal attempts to blunt or deny this and other biblical testimonies to Christ's deity, consult Ronald Nash, *Christianity and the Hellenistic World* (Grand Rapids: Zondervan, 1985).

7. See the New Testament's Epistle to the Hebrews, chapters 8-10.

8. Stott, *Basic Christianity*, p. 96.

9. In Romans 10:9, Paul said that in order for a person to be saved, he or she would have to confess that Jesus was Lord (God) and believe in his or her heart that God has raised Jesus from the dead.

10. Paul lists these appearances in I Corinthians 15:3-8. One of the most enlightening and fascinating books available on this subject is John Wenham's *The Easter Enigma* (Grand Rapids: Zondervan, 1984). For a critical analysis of various attitudes toward the historicity of the resurrection, see Ronald Nash, *Christian Faith and Historical Understanding* (Grand Rapids: Zondervan, 1984), ch. 7.

11. Stott, *Basic Christianity*, p. 61.

12. Ibid.

13. Ibid., pp. 75-76.
14. James I. Packer, *I Want to Be a Christian* (Wheaton, Ill.: Tyndale House, 1977), p. 91.
15. Ibid., p. 92.
16. See William G. McLoughlin, ed., *The American Evangelicals, 1800-1900: An Anthology* (New York: Peter Smith, 1968), 33, 41.
17. John D. Woodbridge, Mark A. Noll, Nathan O. Hatch, *The Gospel in America* (Grand Rapids: Zondervan, 1979), p. 37.

4. The Breakdown of the Orthodox Consensus

1. F. L. Cross and Elizabeth A. Livingstone, ed., *The Oxford Dictionary of the Christian Church* (London: Oxford University Press, 1974), p. 104.
2. Harold O. J. Brown, *Heresies* (Garden City, N.Y.: Doubleday, 1984), p. 417. While Roman Catholicism was able to keep its dissenters in check for a much longer time, the situation today is such that even leading Roman Catholic thinkers can express public doubts about traditional Christian beliefs.
3. For a more complete account, see Ronald Nash, *The Word of God and the Mind of Man* (Grand Rapids: Zondervan, 1982), chapters 1-2.
4. A critical analysis of this chapter in the history of Christian thought can be found in Ronald Nash, *Christian Faith and Historical Understanding* (Grand Rapids: Zondervan, 1984), chapter 2.
5. Brown, *Heresies*, p. 424.

5. Fundamentalism

1. Emilio A. Núñez C., *Liberation Theology* (Chicago: Moody Press, 1985), p. 37.
2. James I. Packer, *Fundamentalism and the Word of God* (Grand Rapids: Eerdmans, 1958), p. 25.
3. Ibid., pp. 25-26.
4. Ibid., p. 32.
5. See Ronald Nash, *The New Evangelicalism* (Grand Rapids: Zondervan, 1963).
6. The Reconstructionist movement is often accused of being schismatic, which may account for its own internal divisions. The individual usually regarded as the founder of the movement is Rousas J. Rushdoony. See his book, *The Foundations of Social Order* (Nutley, N.J. Presbyterian and Reformed, 1972).
7. For an interesting amillennial interpretation of the book of Revelation, see William Hendrickson, *More Than Conquerers* (Grand Rapids: Baker, 1940). For perhaps the most respected critique of the *Scofield Bible* type of dispensationalism, see Oswald T. Allis, *Prophecy and the Church* (Philadelphia: Presbyterian and Reformed, 1945).

8. Jerry Falwell, ed., with Ed Doson and Ed Hindson, *The Fundamentalist Phenomenon* (Garden City, N.Y.: Doubleday, 1981).

9. Ed Dobson, *In Search of Unity* (Nashville: Thomas Nelson, 1985), p. 138.

6. Pentecostalism

1. Margaret M. Poloma, *The Charismatic Movement: Is There a New Pentecost?* (Boston: Twayne, 1982), p. 243.

2. See Richard G. Hutcheson, Jr., *Mainline Churches and the Evangelicals* (Atlanta: John Knox Press, 1981), p. 100.

3. Poloma, *The Charismatic Movement*, p. 243.

4. William G. MacDonald, "Pentecostal Theology: A Classical Viewpoint," in *Perspectives on the New Pentecostalism*, Russell P. Spittler, ed. (Grand Rapids: Baker Book House, 1976), p. 65.

6. Ibid., 15. For a Roman Catholic perspective on Pentecostalism, see Donald L. Felpi, S. J., "Pentecostal Theology: A Roman Catholic Viewpoint," in *Perspectives on the New Pentecostalism*, pp. 87-103. The same book contains another chapter that explains Neo-pentecostalism in more detail: J. Rodman Williams, "Pentecostal Theology: A Neo-Pentecostal Viwpoint," pp. 77-85.

7. MacDonald, "Pentecostal Theology: A Classical Viewpoint," p. 65.

7. Some Representative Evangelicals

1. Tim LaHaye is a noted pastor and author who now heads the American Coalition for Traditional Values in Washington, D.C. He is the author of some twenty books that sell around three hundred thousand copies a year. Greg Dixon is pastor of the Indianapolis Baptist Temple. Dr. Charles Stanley is pastor of the First Baptist Church of Atlanta, Georgia, and president of the Southern Baptist Convention, 1984–1986.

Dr. D. James Kennedy is pastor of the Coral Ridge Presbyterian Church in Fort Lauderdale, Florida, said to be the most rapidly growing Presbyterian church in the nation.

2. For an interesting study of Falwell by a writer outside his movement, see Dinesh D'Souza, *Falwell: Before the Millennium* (Chicago: Regnery Gateway, 1984).

3. Carl F. H. Henry, *God, Revelation and Authority*, 6 vols. (Waco, Texas: Word, 1976–1983). See also Bob E. Patterson, *Carl F. H. Henry* (Waco: Word, 1983).

4. For discussions of views that are very close to Henry's, see Ronald H. Nash, *The Word of God and the Mind of Man* (Grand Rapids: Zondervan, 1982).

5. Francis Schaeffer, *The God Who Is There* (Downers Grove, Ill.: Inter-Varsity Press, 1968) and *Escape from Reason* (Inter-Varsity Press, 1968).

6. Francis A. Schaeffer, *How Should We Then Live?* (Westchester, Ill.: Crossway, 1983).

7. Francis A. Schaeffer and C. Everett Koop, *Whatever Happened to the Human Race?* (Old Tappan, New Jersey: Revell, 1979).

8. For more on Schaeffer, see: Louis Gifford Parkhurst, Jr., *Francis Schaeffer, The Man and His Message* (Wheaton: Tyndale House, 1985); Lane T. Dennis, ed., *Francis Schaeffer: Portraits of the Man and His Work* (Westchester, Ill.: Crossway Books, 1986); and Ronald Ruegsegger, ed., *Reflections on Francis Schaeffer* (Grand Rapids: Zondervan, 1986).

9. The American editions of Lewis's theological writings noted in the text are: *The Problem of Pain* (New York: Macmillan, 1978), *The Screwtape Letters* (New York: Macmillan, 1980), *Mere Christianity* (New York: Macmillan, 1978), and *Miracles: A Preliminary Study* (New York: Macmillan, 1963). Macmillan also published *The Lion, the Witch and the Wardrobe* in 1970.

10. C. S. Lewis, *Mere Christianity*, pp. 55-56.

8. Evangelical Pressure Points

1. Harold Lindsell, *The Battle for the Bible* (Grand Rapids: Zondervan, 1978).

2. For Henry's own views on inerrancy, see Carl F. H. Henry, *God, Revelation and Authority*, vol. 4 (Waco, Texas: Word, 1979), pp. 129-242. There are several aspects to Henry's stand on this issue: (1) Some religious cults (for example, the Jehovah's Witnesses) that are decidedly non-evangelical accept biblical inerrancy. Therefore, an acceptance of inerrancy cannot be the *only* test of true Evangelicalism; (2) nonetheless, Henry maintains, inerrancy is normative for evangelicals; it is a position that evangelicals *should* accept; (3) but Henry believes it is too extreme to say that someone is not really an evangelical if he or she rejects inerrancy while still subscribing to all the great historical creeds; (4) it would be more accurate, Henry thinks, to say that such a person is an inconsistent evangelical.

3. See "The Chicago Statement on Biblical Inerrancy," in *Evangelicals and Inerrancy*, ed. Ronald Youngblood (Nashville: Thomas Nelson, 1984), pp. 230-39.

4. Ibid., p. 231.

5. Ibid., p. 233.

6. Carl Henry, *God, Revelation, and Authority*, vol. 4, p. 354.

7. "The Chicago Statement," p. 234.

8. Ibid., pp. 233-34.

9. For Henry's discussion of ten alleged errors or contradictions in Scripture, see *God, Revelation, and Authority*, vol. 4, pp. 362-64.

10. "The Chicago Statement," pp. 237-38.

11. George E. Ladd, *The New Testament and Criticism* (Grand Rapids: Eerdmans, 1966), p. 381.

12. Carl Henry, *God, Revelation, and Authority*, vol. 4, p. 393.

13. Richard G. Hutcheson, Jr., *Mainline Churches and the Evangelicals* (Atlanta: John Knox Press, 1981), p. 34.

14. The complex nature of evangelical attitudes toward biblical criticism is apparent in several recent studies. See the discussion of form criticism and redaction criticism in Ronald Nash, *Christian Faith and Historical Understanding* (Grand Rapids: Zondervan, 1984), p. 64-75, along with a long bibliographic note on page 167. Also worth consulting is a report of the Christianity Today Institute: "Redaction Criticism: Is It Worth The Risk?" in *Christianity Today*, p. 29 (Oct. 18, 1985).

15. James I. Packer, *Fundamentalism and the Word of God* (Grand Rapids: Eerdmans, 1958), p. 96.

16. See James I. Packer, "The Centrality of Hermeneutics Today," in *Scripture and Truth*, ed. D. A. Carson and John D. Woodbridge (Grand Rapids: Zondervan, 1983), 325-56; and Robert K. Johnston, *The Use of the Bible in Theology: Evangelical Options* (Atlanta: John Knox Press, 1985). Johnston's book contains essays by evangelicals who speak from a variety of perspectives—Clark Pinnock, James Packer, Russell Spittler, Donald Bloesch, John Howard Yoder, Donald Dayton, Robert Webber, William Dyrness, David Wells, and Gabriel Fackre.

17. Robert Johnston provides a good starting point for an examination of evangelical attitudes on feminism and homosexuality. See his book, *Evangelicals at an Impasse* (Atlanta: John Knox Press, 1979). His book contains information about numerous other sources that can be consulted. For a more recent statement of the majority evangelical view on homosexuality, see John Stott, *Social and Sexual Relationships in the Modern World* (Old Tappan: Revell, 1985) and John Stott, "Homosexual Marriage," *Christianity Today* 29 (Nov. 22, 1985), p. 21-28. On national defense and nuclear war, see Philip F. Lawler, ed., *Justice and War in the Nuclear Age* (Lanham, Maryland: University Press of America, 1983). Although the contributors to Lawler's book are Roman Catholics, their position is acceptable to evangelical advocates of the Just War tradition. Lloyd Billingsley has provided a sharp attack on evangelicals who seem to exercise a double standard when comparing their own country with the Soviet Union. See Lloyd Billingsley, *The Generation that Knew Not Josef* (Portland: Multnomah Press, 1985). For an account of the Sandinista movement in Nicaragua by a former Marxist supporter of the Sandinistas, see Humberto Belli, *Breaking Faith* (Westchester, Illinois: Crossway Books, 1985). See also Ronald Nash, ed., *Liberation Theology* (Milford, Michigan: Mott Media, 1984) and Emilio A. Núñez C., *Liberation Theology* (Chicago: Moody Press, 1985).

18. Francis A. Schaeffer and C. Everett Koop, *Whatever Happened to the Human Race?* in *The Complete Works of Francis A. Schaeffer*, vol. 5, second ed. (Westchester, Ill.: Crossway Books, 1985), p. 281.

19. Ibid., pp. 283-84.

20. Ibid., p. 284.

21. See Robert G. Clouse, *The Cross and the Flag* (Carol Stream, Illinois: Creation House, 1972); Richard V. Pierard, *The Unequal Yoke* (Philadelphia: J. B. Lippincott, 1970); and Vernon Grounds, *Evangelicalism and Social Reponsibility* (Scottsdale, PA: Herald Press, 1969).

22. Lloyd Billingsley reviews the *Sojourners'* record on such issues in his book, *The Generation that Knew Not Josef* (Portland: Multnomah Press, 1985).

23. Evangelical theologian, Clark Pinnock, who had been a supporter of the Sojourners' movement from its start, caused some noticeable discomfort when he announced that he could no longer support the magazine's ideology and resigned from its editorial board. Pinnock gives his reasons in his essay, "A Pilgrimage in Political Theology," in *Liberation Theology*, Ronald Nash, ed. (Milford, Mich.: Mott Media, 1984), pp. 103-20.

24. Novak has published extensively in this area. But see his *The Spirit of Democratic Capitalism* (New York: Simon & Schuster, 1982).

25. See Ronald Nash, "The Economics of Justice," *Christianity Today*, p. 23 (March 23, 1979),)24-30; *Freedom, Justice, and the State* (Lanham, Md.: University Press of America, 1980); *Social Justice and the Christian Church* (Milford, Michigan: Mott Media, 1983); "Socialism, Capitalism and the Bible," *Imprimis* 14 (July, 1985); "The Christian Debate Over Economic Freedom," *The Journal of Private Enterprise* 1 (Fall, 1985), 58-64; and *Poverty and Wealth: The Christian Debate Over Capitalism* (Westchester, Illinois: Crossway Books, 1986).

26. See James Gwartney and Thomas S. McCaleb, "Have Anti-poverty Programs Increased Poverty?" *Cato Journal* 4 (1985), pp. 1-16. Gwartney is co-author (with Richard Stroup) of *Economics, Private and Public Choice*, 3rd ed. (Orlando: Academic Press, 1983), one of the most widely used economics texts in the country. See also Charles Murray, *Losing Ground* (New York: Basic Books, 1984).

27. James Gwartney, "Social Progress, the Tax-Transfer Society and the Limits of Public Policy," unpublished paper, Department of Economics, Florida State University, p. 3.

28. Herbert Schlossberg, *Idols for Destruction* (Nashville: Thomas Nelson, 1983), p. 256.

29. Ken Myers, "Biblical Obedience and Political Thought: Some Reflections on Theological Method," to appear as a chapter in a forthcoming book, *Bible, Politics, and Democracy* (Grand Rapids: Eerdmans, 1986), edited by Richard John Neuhaus.

30. Ibid.

31. Ronald Sider, *Rich Christians in an Age of Hunger* (Downers Grove, Illinois: Inter-Varsity Press, 1977).

32. Cullen Murphy, "Protestantism and the Evangelicals," *The Wilson Quarterly* 5 (1981), p. 105.

FOR FURTHER READING

Readers interested in exploring the topics of this book further will find the following books helpful places to begin. Additional works are identified in the notes. Books marked "out of print" are often available at better college or seminary libraries or through interlibrary loan.

Bloesch, Donald G. *The Evangelical Renaissance.* Grand Rapids: Eerdmans, 1973. Out of print.

Carnell, Edward John. (R. Nash, editor). *The Case for Biblical Christianity.* Grand Rapids: Eerdmans, 1969. Out of print.

———. *The Case for Orthodox Theology.* Philadelphia: Westminster Press, 1959. Out of print.

Davis, John J. *Foundations of Evangelical Theology.* Grand Rapids: Baker, 1984.

Dobson, Ed. *In Search of Unity.* Nashville: Thomas Nelson, 1985.

Dennis, Lane T. *Francis Schaeffer: Portraits of the Man and His Work.* Westchester, Ill.: Crossway, 1986.

Falwell, Jerry; Dobson, Ed; and Hindson, Ed, eds. *The Fundamentalist Phenomenon.* Garden City, N.Y.: Doubleday-Galilee, 1980. Out of print.

Henry, Carl F. H., ed. *Basic Christian Doctrines.* Grand Rapids: Baker, no date.

———, ed. *Christian Faith and Modern Theology.* (New York: Channel, 1964. Out of print.

———, ed. *Revelation and the Bible.* Grand Rapids: Baker, 1967.

Johnston, Robert K. *Evangelicals at an Impasse.* Atlanta: John Knox, 1979.

Machen, J. Gresham. *Christianity and Liberalism*. Grand Rapids: Eerdmans, 1923.

Marsden, George, ed. *Evangelicalism and Modern America*. Grand Rapids: Eerdmans, 1984.

Marsden, George. *Fundamentalism and American Culture*. New York: Oxford University Press, 1982.

Nash, Ronald H. *Christian Faith and Historical Understanding*. Grand Rapids: Zondervan, 1984.

———. *Poverty and Wealth: The Christian Debate Over Capitalism*. Westchester, Ill.: Crossway Books, 1986.

———. *Christianity and the Hellenistic World*. Grand Rapids: Zondervan, 1984.

———. *The Concept of God*. Grand Rapids: Zondervan, 1983.

———. *Evangelical Renewal in the Mainline Churches*. Westchester, Ill.: Crossway, 1987.

———. *Freedom, Justice, and the State*. Lanham, Md.: University Press of America, 1980.

———. ed. *Liberation Theology*. Milford, Mich.: Mott, 1984.

———. *The New Evangelicalism*. Grand Rapids: Zondervan, 1963. Out of print.

———. *Process Theology*. Grand Rapids: Baker, 1987.

———. *Social Justice and the Christian Church*. Milford, Mich. Mott, 1983.

Noll, Mark A. and Hatch, Nathan O. *The Search for Christian America*. Westchester, Ill.: Crossway, 1983.

Packer, J. I. *I Want to Be a Christian*. Wheaton, Ill.: Tyndale, 1977.

Patterson, Bob. *Carl F. H. Henry*. Waco, Tex.: Word, 1983.

Quebedeaux, Richard. *The New Charismatics II*. New York: Harper & Row, 1983.

———. *The Young Evangelicals*. New York: Harper & Row, 1974.

Schaeffer, Francis A. *The Complete Works of Francis A. Schaeffer*, 5 vols. Westchester, Ill.: Crossway, 1982.

Schaeffer, Franky. *Bad News for Modern Man*. Westchester, Ill.: Crossway, 1984.

———. ed. *Is Capitalism Christian?* Westchester, Ill.: Crossway, 1985.

Wells, David F. and Woodbridge, John D., eds. *The Evangelicals.* Nashville: Abingdon Press, 1975.

Woodbridge, John D., Noll, Mark A., Hatch, Nathan O. *The Gospel in America* Grand Rapids: Zondervan, 1979. Out of print.

Youngblood, Ronald, ed. *Evangelicals and Inerrancy.* Nashville: Thomas Nelson, 1984.

INDEX